MYSTERY
AND WONDER
Anthology

SERIES EDITORS
Margaret Iveson
Samuel Robinson

EDITORIAL CONSULTANT
Alan Simpson

LITERATURE CONSULTANT
Rivka Cranley

TEACHER CONSULTANTS
Flora Miller
Neil Andersen
John Bebbington
David Crichton
Judy Thorne

PRENTICE HALL CANADA INC.

ISBN 0-13-017088-7

Anthologist: Todd Mercer
Researchers: Monika Croydon, Catherine Rondina

A Ligature, Inc. Book
Cover Illustration: Greg Couch

Canadian Cataloguing in Publication Data

Main entry under title:

Mystery and Wonder: anthology

(MultiSource)
ISBN 0-13-017088-7

1. Fantastic literature. 2. Detective and mystery stories
3. Children's literature. I. Iveson, Margaret L., 1948–
II. Robinson, Sam, 1937–   . III. Series.
PZ5.M97 1993   j808.8'037   C92–094875–8

Printed and bound in Canada

5 6 7 DWF 98 97

"The most beautiful thing we can
experience is the mysterious:
it is the source of all true art
and science."

ALBERT EINSTEIN

Contents

THE
JADE PEONY

Wayson Choy

When Grandmama died at eighty-three our whole household held its breath. She had promised us a sign of her leaving, final proof that her present life had ended well. My parents knew that without any clear sign, our own family fortunes could be altered, threatened. My stepmother looked endlessly into the small cluttered room the ancient lady had occupied. Nothing was touched; nothing changed. My father, thinking that a sign should appear in Grandmama's garden, looked at the frost-killed shoots and cringed: *no, that could not be it.*

My two older teenage brothers and my sister, Liang, age fourteen, were embarrassed by my parents' behavior. What would all the white people in Vancouver think of us? We were Canadians now, *Chinese-Canadians*, a hyphenated reality that my parents could never accept. So it seemed, for different reasons, we all held our breath waiting for *something*.

I was eight when she died. For days she had resisted going into the hospital . . . *a cold, just a cold* . . . and instead gave constant instruction to my stepmother and sister on the boiling of ginseng roots mixed with bitter extract. At night, between wracking coughs and deadly silences, Grandmama had her back and chest rubbed with heated camphor oil and sipped a bluish decoction of an herb called Peacock's Tail. When all these failed to abate her fever, she began to arrange the details of her will. This she did with my father, confessing finally: "I am too stubborn. The only cure for old age is to die."

My father wept to hear this. I stood beside her bed; she turned to me. Her round face looked darker, and the gentleness of her eyes, the thin, arching eyebrows, seemed weary. I brushed the few strands of gray, brittle hair from her face; she managed to smile at me. Being the youngest, I had spent nearly all my time with her and could not imagine that we would ever be parted. Yet when she spoke, and her voice hesitated, cracked, the sombre shadows of her room chilled me. Her wrinkled brow grew wet with fever, and her small body seemed even more diminutive.

"I—I am going to the hospital, Grandson." Her hand reached out for mine. "You know, Little Son, whatever happens I will never leave you." Her palm felt plush and warm, the slender, old fingers boney and firm, so magically strong was her grip that I could not imagine how she could ever part from me. Ever.

Her hands *were* magical. My most vivid memories are of her hands: long, elegant fingers, with impeccable nails, a skein of fine, barely seen veins, and wrinkled skin like light pine. Those hands were quick when she taught me, at six, simple tricks of juggling, learnt when she was a village girl in Southern Canton; a troupe of actors had stayed on her father's farm. One of them, "tall and pale as the whiteness of petals," fell in love with her, promising to return. In her last years his image came back like a third being in our two lives. He had been magician, acrobat, juggler, and some of the things he taught her she had absorbed and passed on to me through her stories and games. But above all, without realizing it then, her hands conveyed to me the quality of their love.

Most marvellous for me was the quick-witted skill her hands revealed in making wind chimes for our birthdays: wind chimes in the likeness of her lost friend's only present to her, made of bits of string and scraps, in the centre of which once hung a precious jade peony. This wondrous gift to her broke apart years ago, in China, but Grandmama kept the jade pendant in a tiny red silk envelope, and kept it always in her pocket, until her death.

These were not ordinary, carelessly made chimes, such as those you now find in our Chinatown stores, whose rattling noises drive you mad. But making her special ones caused dissension in our family, and some shame. Each one that she made was created from a treasure trove of glass fragments and castaway costume jewellery, in the same way that her first wind chime had been made. The problem for the rest of the family was in the fact that Grandmama looked for these treasures wandering the back alleys of Keefer and Pender Streets, peering into our neighbors' garbage cans, chasing away hungry, nervous cats and shouting curses at them.

"All our friends are laughing at us!" Older Brother Jung said at last to my father, when Grandmama was away having tea at Mrs. Lim's.

"We are not poor," Oldest Brother Kiam declared, "yet she and Sek-Lung poke through those awful things as if—" he shoved me in frustration and I stumbled against my sister, "—they were beggars!"

"She will make Little Brother crazy!" Sister Liang said. Without warning, she punched me sharply in the back; I jumped. "You see, look how *nervous* he is!"

I lifted my foot slightly, enough to swing it back and kick Liang in the shin. She yelled and pulled back her fist to punch me again. Jung made a menacing move towards me.

"Stop this, all of you!" My father shook his head in exasperation. How could he dare tell the Grand Old One, his aging mother, that what was somehow appropriate in a poor village in China, was an abomination here? How could he prevent me, his youngest, from accompanying her? If she went walking into those alley-ways alone she could well be attacked by hoodlums. "She is not a beggar looking for food. She is searching for—for . . ."

My stepmother attempted to speak, then fell silent. She, too, seemed perplexed and somewhat ashamed. They all loved Grandmama, but she was *inconvenient*, unsettling.

As for our neighbors, most understood Grandmama to be harmlessly crazy, others that she did indeed make lovely toys but for what purpose? *Why?* they asked, and the stories she told me, of the juggler who smiled at her, flashed in my head.

Finally, by their cutting remarks, the family did exert enough pressure so that Grandmama and I no longer openly announced our expeditions. Instead, she took me with her on "shopping trips," ostensibly for clothes or groceries, while in fact we spent most of our time exploring stranger and more distant neighborhoods, searching for splendid junk: jangling pieces of a vase, cranberry glass fragments embossed with leaves, discarded glass beads from Woolworth necklaces . . . We would sneak them all home in brown rice sacks, folded into small parcels, and put them under her bed. During the day when the family was away at school or work, we brought them out and washed every item in a large black pot of boiling lye and water, dried them quickly, carefully, and returned them, sparkling, under her bed.

Our greatest excitement occurred when a fire gutted the large Chinese Presbyterian Church, three blocks from our house. Over the still-smoking ruins the next day, Grandmama and I rushed precariously over the blackened beams to pick out the stained glass that glittered in the sunlight. Small figure bent over, wrapped against the autumn cold in a dark blue quilted coat, happily gathering each piece like gold, she became my spiritual playmate: "There's a good one! *There!*"

Hours later, soot-covered and smelling of smoke, we came home with a carton full of delicate fragments, still early enough to steal them all into the house and put the small box under her bed. "These are special pieces," she said, giving the box a last push, "because they come from a sacred place." She slowly got up and I saw, for the first time, her hand begin to shake. But then, in her joy, she embraced me. Both of our hearts were racing, as if we were two dreamers. I buried my face in her blue quilt, and for a moment, the whole world seemed silent.

"My juggler," she said, "he never came back to me from Honan . . . perhaps the famine . . ." Her voice began to quake. "But I shall have my sacred wind chime . . . I shall have it again."

One evening, when the family was gathered in their usual places in the parlor, Grandmama gave me her secret nod: a slight wink of her eye and a flaring of her nostrils. There was *trouble* in the air. Supper had gone badly, school examinations were due. Father had failed to meet an editorial deadline at the *Vancouver Chinese Times*. A huge sigh came from Sister Liang.

"But it is useless this Chinese they teach you!" she lamented, turning to Stepmother for support. Silence. Liang frowned, dejected, and went back to her Chinese book, bending the covers back.

"Father," Oldest Brother Kiam began, waving his bamboo brush in the air, "you must realize that this Mandarin only confuses us. We are Cantonese speakers. . . ."

"And you do not complain about Latin, French or German in your English school?" Father rattled his newspaper, a signal that his patience was ending.

"But, Father, those languages are *scientific*." Kiam jabbed his brush in the air. "We are now in a scientific, logical world."

Father was silent. We could all hear Grandmama's rocker.

"What about Sek-Lung?" Older Brother Jung pointed angrily at me. "He was sick last year, but this year he should have at least started Chinese school, instead of picking over garbage cans!"

"He starts next year," Father said, in a hard tone that immediately warned everyone to be silent. Liang slammed her book.

Grandmama went on rocking quietly in her chair. She complimented my mother on her knitting, made a remark about the "strong beauty" of Kiam's brushstrokes which, in spite of himself, immensely pleased him. All this babbling noise was her family torn and confused in a strange land: everything here was so very foreign and scientific.

The truth was, I was sorry not to have started school the year before. In my innocence I had imagined going to school meant certain privileges worthy of all my brothers' and sister's complaints. The fact that my lung infection in my fifth and sixth years, mistakenly diagnosed as TB, earned me some reprieve, only made me long for school the more. Each member of the family took turns on Sunday, teaching me or annoying me. But it was the countless hours I spent with Grandmama that were my real education. Tapping me on my head she would say, "Come, Sek-Lung, we have *our* work," and we would walk up the stairs to her small crowded room. There, in the midst of her antique shawls, the old ancestral calligraphy and multi-colored embroidered hangings, beneath the mysterious shelves of sweet herbs and bitter potions, we would continue doing what we had started that morning: the elaborate wind chime for her death.

"I can't last forever," she declared, when she let me in on the secret of this one. "It will sing and dance and glitter," her long fingers stretched into the air, pantomiming the waving motion of her ghost chimes: "My spirit will hear its sounds and see its light and return to this house and say goodbye to you."

Deftly she reached into the carton she had placed on the chair beside me. She picked out a fish-shape amber piece, and with a long needle-like tool and a steel ruler, she scored it. Pressing the blade of a cleaver against the line, with the fingers of her other hand, she lifted up the glass until it cleanly *snapped* into the exact shape she required. Her hand began to tremble, the tips of her fingers to shiver, like rippling water.

"You see that, Little One?" She held her hand up. "That is my body fighting with Death. He is in this room now."

My eyes darted in panic, but Grandmama remained calm, undisturbed, and went on with her work. Then I remembered the glue and uncorked the jar for her. Soon the graceful ritual movements of her hand returned to her, and I became lost in the magic of her task: she dabbed a cabalistic mixture of glue on one end and skillfully dropped the braided end of a silk thread into it. This part always amazed me: the braiding would slowly, *very* slowly, *unknot*, fanning out like a prized fishtail. In a few seconds the clear, homemade glue began to harden as I blew lightly over it, welding to itself each separate silk strand.

Each jam-sized pot of glue was precious: each large cork had been wrapped with a fragment of pink silk. I remember this part vividly, because each cork was treated to a special rite. First we went shopping in the best silk stores in Chinatown for the perfect square of silk she required. It had to be a deep pink, a shade of color blushing toward red. And the tone had to match—as closely as possible—her precious jade carving, the small peony of white and light-red jade, her most lucky possession. In the centre of this semi-translucent carving, no more than an inch wide, was a pool of pink light, its veins swirling out into the petals of the flower.

"This color is the color of my spirit," she said, holding it up to the window so I could see the delicate pastel against the broad strokes of sunlight. She dropped her voice, and I held my breath at the wonder of the color. "This was given to me by the young actor who taught me how to juggle. He had four of them, and each one had a centre of this rare color, the color of Good Fortune." The pendant seemed to pulse as she turned it: "Oh, Sek-Lung! He had white hair and white skin *to his toes! It's true.* I saw him bathing." She laughed and blushed, her eyes softened at the memory. The silk had to match the pink heart of her pendant: the color was magical for her, to hold the unravelling strands of her memory . . .

It was just six months before she died that we really began to work on her last wind chime. Three thin bam-

boo sticks were steamed and bent into circlets: thirty
exact lengths of silk thread, the strongest kind, were cut
and braided at both ends and glued to stained glass. Her
hands worked on their own command, each hand racing
with a life of its own: cutting, snapping, braiding, knotting . . . Sometimes she breathed heavily and her small
body, growing thinner, sagged against me. *Death*, I
thought. *He is in this room*, and I would work harder
alongside her. For months Grandmama and I did this
every other evening, a half dozen pieces each time. The
shaking in her hand grew worse, but we said nothing.
Finally, after discarding hundreds, she told me she had the
necessary thirty pieces. But this time, because it was a
sacred chime, I would not be permitted to help her tie it
up or have the joy of raising it. "Once tied," she said,
holding me against my disappointment, "not even I can
raise it. Not a sound must it make until I have died."

"What will happen?"

"Your father will then take the centre braided strand
and raise it. He will hang it against my bedroom window
so that my ghost may see it, and hear it, and return. I
must say goodbye to this world properly or wander in
this foreign land forever."

"You can take the streetcar!" I blurted, suddenly
shocked that she actually meant to leave me. I thought I
could hear the clear chromatic chimes, see the shimmer-
ing colors on the wall: I fell against her and cried, and
there in my crying I knew that she would die. I can still
remember the touch of her hand on my head, and the
smell of her thick woolen sweater pressed against my
face. "I will always be with you, Little Sek-Lung, but in a
different way . . . you'll see."

Months went by, and nothing happened. Then one
late September evening, when I had just come home from

Chinese School, Grandmama was preparing supper when she looked out our kitchen window and saw a cat—a long, lean white cat—jump into our garbage pail and knock it over. She ran out to chase it away, shouting curses at it. She did not have her thick sweater on and when she came back into the house, a chill gripped her. She leaned against the door: "That was not a cat," she said, and the odd tone of her voice caused my father to look with alarm at her. "I can not take back my curses. It is too late." She took hold of my father's arm: "It was all white and had pink eyes like sacred fire."

My father started at this, and they both looked pale. My brothers and sister, clearing the table, froze in their gestures.

"The fog has confused you," Stepmother said. "It was just a cat."

But Grandmama shook her head, for she knew it was a sign. "I will not live forever," she said. "I am prepared."

The next morning she was confined to her bed with a severe cold. Sitting by her, playing with some of my toys, I asked her about the cat: "Why did Father jump at the cat with the pink eyes? He didn't see it, you did."

"But he and your mother know what it means."

"What?"

"My friend, the juggler, the magician, was as pale as white jade, and he had pink eyes." I thought she would begin to tell me one of her stories, a tale of enchantment or of a wondrous adventure, but she only paused to swallow; her eyes glittered, lost in memory. She took my hand, gently opening and closing her fingers over it. "Sek-Lung," she sighed, "*he* has come back to me."

Then Grandmama sank back into her pillow and the embroidered flowers lifted to frame her wrinkled face. I saw her hand over my own, and my own began to tremble. I fell fitfully asleep by her side. When I woke up it was dark and her bed was empty. She had been taken to the hospital and I was not permitted to visit.

A few days after that she died of the complications of pneumonia. Immediately after her death my father came home and said nothing to us, but walked up the stairs to her room, pulled aside the drawn lace curtains of her window and lifted the wind chimes to the sky.

I began to cry and quickly put my hand in my pocket for a handkerchief. Instead, caught between my fingers, was the small, round firmness of the jade peony. In my mind's eye I saw Grandmama smile and heard, softly, the pink centre beat like a beautiful, cramped heart.

Southern Mansion

Poplars are standing there still as death
and ghosts of dead men
meet their ladies walking
two by two beneath the shade
and standing on the marble steps.

There is a sound of music echoing
through the open door
and in the field there is
another sound tinkling in the cotton:
chains of bondmen dragging on the ground.

The years go back with an iron clank,
a hand is on the gate,
a dry leaf trembles on the wall.
Ghosts are walking.
They have broken roses down
and poplars stand there still as death.

ARNA BONTEMPS

WAS IT MURDER?

Cheryl MacDonald

On the evening of 13 August 1896 a sad little group disembarked from the Grand Trunk Railway train at Cayuga, Ontario. Olive Sternaman, a neat, slim woman in her late twenties, helped her two young sons off the train, then, her face creased with worry, watched as brakeman Albert Cox assisted her husband to the ground. Since leaving Buffalo, George had lain on a cot in the baggage car, unable to sit or stand. He had been ailing since June. With his income as a carpenter cut off, the family had no money to pay the rent. So George had written to his mother, asking to come home to her with his wife and stepsons.

For Olive, the decision to move to Canada was not an easy one. True, she had been born nearby and still had relatives in the area, but there was no love lost between Olive and her mother-in-law, Eliza Sternaman. All the same, the two women were prepared to tolerate each other for George's sake.

George's brother Avery, a neighbour, Peter Hunsinger, and Eliza had driven a wagon to the station. The ride over country roads from Cayuga to the third concession, Rainham Township, was agonizing for George, who felt every bump and jolt, and nearly as painful for the others, who could do nothing to help. No one was in any mood to appreciate the quiet beauty of the countryside as the wagon climbed the long hill out of the Grand River valley and turned southwards toward Lake Erie.

It was dark when the wagon reached the Sternaman house. The men carried George into the house, to a bedroom just inside the front door. He was barely settled before the first disagreement between Olive and her mother-in-law occurred. The doctor in Buffalo had warned against the journey, and Olive wanted a physician's reassurance that no harm had been done. But Eliza Sternaman had not sent for a doctor. After a brief discussion, she agreed to call one in the next day.

When Dr. Phillip Park of Fisherville arrived the following morning, he insisted on being alone with his patient. He found George terribly emaciated, with a weak and rapid pulse. There were white patches and ulcers inside his mouth. His legs were paralyzed, and he could barely move his arms. After questioning him about his drinking habits, Park came to a horrifying conclusion: George was suffering from arsenic poisoning.

Outside the sick room, Dr. Park spoke to Olive, asking whether George had any enemies in Buffalo, anyone who might have given him a "poisonous draught." No, Olive told him, adding he was the first doctor to suggest poisoning.

Unwilling to trust his own judgement in a case with such serious implications, Park asked Olive if he might bring in another, more experienced physician, and suggested Dr. T. T. S. Harrison of Selkirk. Olive agreed to Harrison, who had once been the Sternaman family physician, was highly respected locally, and had recently served as the president of the Canadian Medical Association.

Dr. Harrison's diagnosis confirmed Park's. There was no doubt that George was suffering from arsenic poisoning, but Park's tests indicated that the poison had not been administered for some time. Park prescribed medicine that was supposed to clear arsenic from the system, but it was far too late. On 19 August George died. Later that day, Park and Harrison returned to perform one last grisly duty.

Several weeks earlier, George had requested an autopsy in the event of his death. One of the reasons he felt compelled to do so was the mysterious circumstances surrounding the demise of Olive's first husband, Ezra Elam Chipman, and the similarities between Chipman's and his own illness.

Like George, Chipman was a Canadian, a carpenter from St. Catharines. In Buffalo, he had worked hard, rose to the position of foreman, and, because he always brought his money home, was better off than many of his peers. In 1894, having met young George Sternaman on a construction site, Chipman invited him to board with the family.

The three adults got on quite well, even making trips to visit friends and relatives in southern Ontario together. Then, shortly before Christmas 1894 Elam Chipman fell ill on the job. Workmates saw him toss away an unfinished piece of pie. "I guess the old woman has seasoned it with cayenne pepper instead of spice," he joked. Soon, he was complaining. "My stomach is burning to pieces." He was terribly thirsty, and began to vomit violently. Confined to bed, he eventually became paralyzed, and on 20 January 1895 died of "multiple neuritis." Many said he had been poisoned.

George's behaviour did not help quell the gossip. Olive kept Elam's photograph on an easel in the front parlour. Whenever George saw it, he would fly into a rage, insisting that it be covered. Although his mother tried to change his mind, he continued to live with Olive and her two sons. Soon he was courting the widow, and by September told his mother of his intentions to marry her. Eliza Sternaman was furious. "You'll be dead in six months," she warned.

Olive and George were married in Buffalo on 3 February 1896. In June, George took sick at work, just as Elam had done. A succession of doctors treated him, and, although George seemed to be mending at one point, by late July he was obviously failing. Around this time, the family's lack of income forced the move to Canada, where George succumbed to his illness.

Harrison and Park looked for arsenic in the autopsy. When their tests proved inconclusive Harrison suggested the cause of death be listed as multiple neuritis arising from paralysis, the same symptoms which preceded Elam Chipman's death. He also recommended that the body be tampered with as little as possible. As he told undertaker John Snyder, they hadn't heard the last of the case.

While Snyder made the funeral arrangements, Eliza broached the subject of insurance. Until Olive and George were married, she had been the beneficiary of his insurance policies, but within days of the wedding, the policies had been changed in Olive's favour. Now, Eliza wanted to know how much insurance her daughter-in-law could expect, and when she would claim the money. Olive told her there were a few hundred dollars in the Carpenters' Union, but a second policy had been allowed to lapse. As for applying for the money, Olive told her mother-in-law, "My Ma has already done so."

As soon as the funeral was over, Olive returned to Buffalo with her two boys, where they all moved into the home of Elam's mother. In September, a letter from Eliza arrived. Since Olive had received the insurance money, Eliza felt justified in asking for $25. The money, she said, would cover the cost of feeding the couple during George's final days, as well as compensate his brothers, Avery and Freeman, for running errands. On the advice of friends, Olive ignored the letter, much to Eliza's annoyance.

In September, the minister of the Baptist Church, John Trickey, called on Eliza. He had received a request to supply a burial certificate to an American insurance company. Apparently, George had more insurance than Olive admitted to. For Eliza, this was the last straw. She called on C. W. Coulter, Haldimand County's crown attorney, explaining her suspicions. Coulter referred the matter to coroner David Thompson.

Thompson called an inquest into the death of George Sternaman. While Freeman Sternaman, John Snyder, and Doctors Park and Harrison looked on, George's body was exhumed and carried to Rainham Township Hall. There, Harrison and Park performed another autopsy, sealing several organs in glass bottles to ship to William Ellis, a University of Toronto chemistry professor who carried out forensic investigations for the provincial government. Park and Harrison also testified to their findings, the circumstances surrounding George's death, and the fact that the body had been remarkably well preserved.

Alerted to the mysterious goings-on in Haldimand County, provincial detective John Wilson Murray arrived on the scene. Strong, silent, stubborn and fearless, a contemporary described him as a "faithful friend and relentless foe." Those attributes served him well as a detective for the Ontario Police Force, which he joined in 1875.

Initially, Murray thought the suspicions against Olive were unfounded and that the case "would end in a fizzle." After some investigation, he changed his opinion, concluding Olive had poisoned both her husbands. Particularly damning was a letter written on 10 June 1896:

> To all whom it may concern,
>
> I, Geo. H. Sternaman having had very peculiar attacks at times during the past 6 mos and of which no one but my wife and a few of her relatives know anything of, write this to state that if I should die while in one of them that no person can say that it was by her hands in any way that I died. . . .

Murray pointed out the similarities between the handwriting in the letter and Olive's. Moreover, it was discovered that along with the insurance from the Carpenters' Union, George also had $1,770 insurance in other companies. Her deception about the insurance along with the circumstances of Elam's death and Dr. Ellis's discovery of arsenic in George's viscera convinced authorities to issue a warrant for Olive's arrest.

She was taken into custody in Buffalo on 27 October. Because George had died in Canada, Canadian authorities felt extradition was in order, and a hearing got under way. As doctors, insurance agents and others testified, Olive sat calmly in the Buffalo courtroom. At first, she seemed unconcerned, but as the hearing continued, she became more worried. On 17 November she "gave way to hysterical weeping" when her lawyer, Wallace Thayer, described George's death.

Still, she was sure she would be acquitted. On the morning of 4 December, looking calm and hopeful, she was escorted into the courtroom. Commissioner Fairchild read his decision:

> After a very careful examination and hearing of a
> great amount of testimony in this case . . . I deem the
> evidence herein sufficient to sustain the charge . . .

Olive half-rose in her chair, flushed and smiling. She
and others in the courtroom had understood "here insuf-
ficient" but as Fairchild continued, the mistake became
apparent. Her face fell, but she did not weep or protest.

Olive wanted to return to Canada to stand trial as
soon as possible. Friends and her lawyer advised against
it. In all likelihood, she was told, the trial would be at the
Haldimand County Courthouse in Cayuga, where public
feeling would be against her. As a consequence, the extradition order was appealed, first in New York State, and
finally in Washington. Fairchild's decision stood. In the
late summer of 1897, more than a year after George's
death, John Murray escorted Olive to Cayuga.

The trial began on 17 November with Judge Armour
presiding. William Manley German, a Welland lawyer
and politician, represented Olive. The crown prosecutor
was Britton Bath Osler, older brother of the famous
physician, William. "Brick" Osler was considered the best
criminal lawyer of the day, a gifted orator and logical
thinker who was frequently called on to protect the
Crown's interests in civil and criminal trials.

Much of the evidence was already known to the
spectators who jammed the Cayuga court house, for the
proceedings of the extradition hearing had been widely
publicized. A parade of doctors testified, including
William Ellis, who made it clear that the body of George
Sternaman had contained lethal quantities of arsenic. The
crucial question was how had the poison got there? Neither John Snyder nor his son and apprentice Abraham
were reliable witnesses. They claimed the body had not
been embalmed, but both Olive's sister Lizzie and her

aunt testified that Snyder had told them the cost of the funeral included the cost of embalming. John Chevalier of Selkirk told of meeting Snyder in Ivan W. Holmes' general store, where the undertaker boasted that the results of the inquest would depend on what he said in the witness box. When Chevalier asked if he had embalmed the body, Snyder replied, "We always embalm."

The evidence regarding insurance was most telling. There were three policies, and the agents who collected the premiums on a weekly basis claimed the money was invariably paid by Olive herself. Furthermore, she was extremely secretive about the policies. J. E. Dow, the insurance agent for John Hancock Mutual, said he met Olive on Dearborn Street in Buffalo. She was in mourning, and he stopped to ask about George's death. Olive told him a few details, then asked him not to say anything about the $1,000 life insurance policy. If her mother, father and sisters learned about it, she said, they would get it from her in a short time.

As Brick Osler himself admitted, all the evidence was circumstantial. But skillful presentation on the part of the Crown prosecutor quickly built the case against Olive, and her own behaviour helped cement the evidence in place. Although everyone, including her vindictive mother-in-law, agreed that she was a singularly devoted and affectionate wife to George, they also testified to contradictory remarks she had made. Two of the Buffalo doctors who examined George told her they suspected poison, but she had not thought it necessary to mention the fact to Dr. Park after returning to Canada. And, although she sometimes gave way to weeping while in the Buffalo and Cayuga courtrooms, such displays of grief were exceptional. In fact, moments before her trial began, she was joking with women friends in the courtroom, and she usually sat placidly listening to evidence as though it had no power to affect her. For some, this was proof of her cold-blooded and murderous nature.

William German did what he could to lessen the impact of the evidence. In his summing up, he argued that unless Olive was a "fiend from hell" she had no motive for murdering George, nor, for that matter, her first husband. Both men had brought in good wages, and the profits from the insurance were minimal.

Osler presented his final arguments, then Judge Armour made his charge to the jury. The twelve men, most of whom were farmers, left to consider the evidence at 4:40 p.m. Four hours later, they filed back into the room. "Your Lordship," the jury foreman asked, "what power have we as to any recommendation to mercy?"

"You can recommend to mercy if you think fit," Armour replied.

Olive was sent for. Pale but calm, she arrived from the jail and took her place in the dock.

The court was heavily shadowed, lit only by a few smoking lamps. Judge Armour sat in the glare of one, while Olive was half hidden in the gloom. The jury foreman walked from the box and handed the verdict to the judge. Armour unfolded the paper. "Gentlemen of the jury," he cried, "hearken to your verdict as the court records it, a verdict of guilty, so say you all."

Some women in the gallery moaned. Others strained to watch as Armour ordered Olive to stand. "What have you to say that the sentence of the court should not be pronounced upon you?"

Pale but still controlled, Olive rose. "I am not guilty." Her voice was clear, as she looked at the judge she hesitated, then continued. "In the eyes of God I will have a new trial and be acquitted."

Sternly, Armour told her she had had a fair trial, then passed sentence: "That you be taken hence to the place whence you came, and that you be thence taken on Thursday, the twentieth of January next, to the place of execution, and that you be there hanged by the neck until you are dead." His voice quavered. "And may the Lord have mercy on your soul."

A female spectator fainted. Another cried out, while Olive protested, "Oh judge, is there no justice in this country?" Jailer John Murphy and Chief Constable Farrell led her back to the cell.

It had been more than twenty years since a woman had been executed in Ontario, and many were opposed. By the next night, a petition had been started asking that Olive be granted a new trial. Among the signatures were those of several members of the jury, who publicly stated that they would not have convicted if they had known Olive would receive a death sentence.

Among Olive's most outspoken advocates were a journalist, Phillips Thompson, and a minister, John G. Foote. A socialist and champion of the working class, Thompson interviewed Olive for newspapers and conducted a campaign in her favour through letters to the editor. (Thompson's grandson, Pierre Berton, would later carry on the family's journalistic tradition.)

Reverend Foote, Cayuga's Methodist minister, had visited Olive regularly during her confinement, and was convinced of her innocence. In conversations and letters to newspapers, he pushed for a new trial. In December, the case was appealed at Osgoode Hall, Toronto, but the verdict was upheld. There seemed little hope; however, William German prepared to make a final appeal to Ottawa.

Foote accompanied him. Together, they called on David Mills, only recently appointed Minister of Justice.

A scholarly man from London, Mills was an expert o. constitutional law who had taught at the University of Toronto. He promised to consider the case carefully. With a committee of fellow cabinet ministers, he reviewed the facts, then presented it to the cabinet as a whole. Mills had two options: he could commute Olive's sentence to life imprisonment, or grant a new trial. After a daylong discussion with the cabinet, he chose the latter option, the first time this was ever done under a new clause in the Criminal Code.

Word reached Cayuga on 18 January 1898. Hangman Radcliffe had just arrived, and the scaffold was being erected in the jail yard when Olive learned the news. Overwhelmed at first, she soon recovered. Her belief that she would be granted a new trial had been vindicated; now, she was convinced, it was only a matter of time before she was proved innocent.

The public interest generated by the trial and death sentence continued. In Buffalo, there were accusations that the Canadian trial had been unfair. In Canada, Olive's supporters argued that, since the government had virtually limitless funds at its disposal, it was able to hire the best lawyers. Olive, who was practically destitute, had to rely on charity. A fund was started to pay for her defence, with groups of supporters banding together in Haldimand County, in Buffalo and Toronto to raise the $500 required.

The second trial got underway in May. Again, Osler represented the Crown. Chancellor John Boyd presided, and Olive's new defence attorney was E. F. B. Johnston of Toronto. A prominent criminal lawyer, Johnston was Osler's chief rival. The two had locked horns at several murder trials, and, in the last two instances, Johnston had won.

In Cayuga, Johnston deftly persuaded witnesses to

express doubts about what they had seen or heard, effectively weakening the evidence against Olive. Late on the evening of 7 May the jury brought in a verdict of not guilty.

The courtroom broke into shouting and cheers. Moments later, as the noise subsided, Boyd ordered Olive to rise. She was flushed and crying, so overcome she could barely stand. Once outside the courtroom, though, she recovered enough to give brief interviews to reporters before her family swept her away to some much-needed privacy in Rainham Township.

But Olive's acquittal was not the end of her ordeal. Although she told some reporters that she had no intention of touching the insurance companies' "dirty money," she had little choice. She had already signed papers agreeing to pay Wallace Thayer and William German's fees from the policies. So, as soon as she returned to Buffalo, she launched a lawsuit against Metropolitan Life. It was quickly dismissed on the grounds that George Sternaman had misrepresented the condition of his health to the company doctor. Wallace Thayer launched an appeal, and a series of courtroom battles began. On the one hand, the company argued that Olive had no claim on the insurance money, since she had been convicted of murder. On the other, her lawyer argued, she had been exonerated. After five trials, the case was finally settled in 1905. Olive got the $1,000, plus costs, all of which went to her lawyers.

Shortly after she regained her freedom, Olive married her third husband. According to one story, the man complained of intestinal problems one day after dinner. Fully aware of his wife's past, he warned her that if he ever felt ill again after eating a meal she had prepared he would kill her himself. They were divorced a short time later.

Olive eventually resumed the name of her first husband and slipped into obscurity. By the time she died in

1941 most people had forgotten the notorious Sternaman poisoning case. But one question was never answered: how did George die? There is little doubt that arsenic was responsible, but how—and by whom—was it administered? Assuming that Olive was innocent, two theories from the murder trials suggest possible answers. The first was accidental poisoning. One of the medications George received contained traces of arsenic; an error by a doctor or pharmacist might have turned those "traces" into a deadly dosage.

However, accidental poisoning ignores the fact of Elam Chipman's death. Circumstantial evidence presented at the trials proved that Olive had the motive, means and opportunity to murder both husbands. However, George Sternaman had the same means and opportunity. As for motive, Olive's mother and sister testified that George became infatuated with Olive while Elam was still alive, and his violent reaction to Elam's photograph suggests jealousy or a guilty conscience. Furthermore, one of the doctors testified George was nervous, excitable, neurotic. Olive spoke of the spells George suffered when he was angry and upset, when he would sit for hours at a time, staring and unresponsive. Once, when George was in one of these spells, she muttered, "Merciful God, if Elam could know I married George and he had these fits he would wish him dead a dozen times."

Was Olive Sternaman an innocent victim of circumstance or a Victorian black widow? No one will ever know for certain.

Trifles

Susan Glaspell

CHARACTERS
GEORGE HENDERSON, County Attorney
HENRY PETERS, Sheriff
LEWIS HALE, a neighboring farmer
MRS. PETERS
MRS. HALE

SCENE: *The kitchen in the now abandoned farmhouse of* JOHN WRIGHT, *a gloomy kitchen, and left without having been put in order—unwashed pans under the sink, a loaf of bread outside the breadbox, a dish towel on the table—other signs of incompleted work. At the rear the outer door opens and the* SHERIFF *comes in followed by the* COUNTY ATTORNEY *and* HALE. *The* SHERIFF *and* HALE *are men in middle life, the* COUNTY ATTORNEY *is a young man; all are much bundled up and go at once to the stove. They are followed by the two women—the* SHERIFF's *wife first; she*

is a slight wiry woman, a thin nervous face. MRS.
HALE *is larger and would ordinarily be called more
comfortable looking, but she is disturbed now and
looks fearfully about as she enters. The women have
come in slowly, and stand close together near the door.*

COUNTY ATTORNEY (*rubbing his hands*). This feels good.
Come up to the fire, ladies.

MRS. PETERS (*after taking a step forward*). I'm not—cold.

SHERIFF (*unbuttoning his overcoat and stepping away
from the stove as if to mark the beginning of official
business*). Now, Mr. Hale, before we move things
about, you explain to Mr. Henderson just what you
saw when you came here yesterday morning.

COUNTY ATTORNEY. By the way, has anything been
moved? Are things just as you left them yesterday?

SHERIFF (*looking about*). It's just the same. When it
dropped below zero last night I thought I'd better
send Frank out this morning to make a fire for us—no
use getting pneumonia with a big case on, but I told
him not to touch anything except the stove—and you
know Frank.

COUNTY ATTORNEY. Somebody should have been left here
yesterday.

SHERIFF. Oh—yesterday. When I had to send Frank to
Morris Center for that man who went crazy—I want
you to know I had my hands full yesterday. I knew
you could get back from Omaha by today and as long
as I went over everything here myself—

COUNTY ATTORNEY. Well, Mr. Hale, tell just what happened when you came here yesterday morning.

HALE. Harry and I had started to town with a load of
potatoes. We came along the road from my place and
as I got here I said, "I'm going to see if I can't get

John Wright to go in with me on a party telephone."
I spoke to Wright about it once before and he put me
off, saying folks talked too much anyway, and all he
asked was peace and quiet—I guess you know about
how much he talked himself; but I thought maybe if I
went to the house and talked about it before his wife,
though I said to Harry that I didn't know as what his
wife wanted made much difference to John—

COUNTY ATTORNEY. Let's talk about that later, Mr. Hale.
I do want to talk about that, but tell now just what
happened when you got to the house.

HALE. I didn't hear or see anything; I knocked at the door,
and still it was all quiet inside. I knew they must be
up, it was past eight o'clock. So I knocked again, and
I thought I heard somebody say, "Come in." I wasn't
sure. I'm not sure yet, but I opened the door—this
door (*indicating the door by which the two women
are still standing*) and there in that rocker—(*pointing
to it*) sat Mrs. Wright.

(*They all look at the rocker.*)

COUNTY ATTORNEY. What—what was she doing?

HALE. She was rockin' back and forth. She had her apron
in her hand and was kind of—pleating it.

COUNTY ATTORNEY. And how did she—look?

HALE. Well, she looked queer.

COUNTY ATTORNEY. How do you mean—queer?

HALE. Well, as if she didn't know what she was going to
do next. And kind of done up.[1]

COUNTY ATTORNEY. How did she seem to feel about your
coming?

---

[1] **done up:** exhausted

HALE. Why, I don't think she minded—one way or other. She didn't pay much attention. I said, "How do, Mrs. Wright, it's cold, ain't it?" And she said, "Is it?"—and went on kind of pleating at her apron. Well, I was surprised; she didn't ask me to come up to the stove, or to set down, but just sat there, not even looking at me, so I said, "I want to see John." And then she— laughed. I guess you would call it a laugh. I thought of Harry and the team outside, so I said a little sharp: "Can't I see John?" "No," she says, kind o' dull like. "Ain't he home?" says I. "Yes," says she, "he's home." "Then why can't I see him?" I asked her, out of patience. "Cause he's dead," says she. "*Dead?*" says I. She just nodded her head, not getting a bit excited, but rockin' back and forth. "Why—where is he?" says I, not knowing what to say. She just pointed upstairs—like that (*himself pointing to the room above*). I got up, with the idea of going up there. I walked from there to here—then I says, "Why, what did he die of?" "He died of a rope round his neck," says she, and just went on pleatin' at her apron. Well, I went out and called Harry. I thought I might—need help. We went upstairs and there he was lyin'—

COUNTY ATTORNEY. I think I'd rather have you go into that upstairs, where you can point it all out. Just go on now with the rest of the story.

HALE. Well, my first thought was to get that rope off. It looked. . . (*stops, his face twitches*). . . but Harry, he went up to him, and he said, "No, he's dead all right, and we'd better not touch anything." So we went back downstairs. She was still sitting that same way. "Has anybody been notified?" I asked. "No," says she, unconcerned. "Who did this, Mrs. Wright?" said Harry. He said it businesslike—and she stopped

pleatin' of her apron. "I don't know," she says. "You
don't *know*?" says Harry. "No," says she. "Weren't
you sleepin' in the bed with him?" says Harry. "Yes,"
says she, "but I was on the inside." "Somebody
slipped a rope round his neck and strangled him and
you didn't wake up?" says Harry. "I didn't wake up,"
she said after him. We must 'a' looked as if we didn't
see how that could be, for after a minute she said,
"I sleep sound." Harry was going to ask her more
questions but I said maybe we ought to let her tell her
story first to the coroner, or the sheriff, so Harry went
fast as he could to Rivers' place, where there's a telephone.

COUNTY ATTORNEY. And what did Mrs. Wright do when
she knew that you had gone for the coroner?

HALE. She moved from that chair to this one over here
(*pointing to a small chair in the corner*) and just sat
there with her hands held together and looking down.
I got a feeling that I ought to make some conversation, so I said I had come in to see if John wanted to
put in a telephone, and at that she started to laugh,
and then she stopped and looked at me—scared.
(*The* COUNTY ATTORNEY, *who has had his notebook
out, makes a note*.) I dunno, maybe it wasn't scared.
I wouldn't like to say it was. Soon Harry got back,
and then Dr. Lloyd came, and you, Mr. Peters, and so
I guess that's all I know that you don't.

COUNTY ATTORNEY (*looking around*). I guess we'll go
upstairs first—and then out to the barn and around
there. (*To the* SHERIFF) You're convinced that there
was nothing important here—nothing that would
point to any motive?

SHERIFF. Nothing here but kitchen things.

(*The* COUNTY ATTORNEY, *after again looking around*

the kitchen, opens the door of a cupboard closet. He gets up on a chair and looks on a shelf. Pulls his hand away, sticky.)

COUNTY ATTORNEY. Here's a nice mess.

(*The women draw nearer.*)

MRS. PETERS (*to the other woman*). Oh, her fruit; it did freeze. (*To the* COUNTY ATTORNEY) She worried about that when it turned so cold. She said the fire'd go out and her jars would break.

SHERIFF. Well, can you beat the women! Held for murder and worryin' about her preserves.

COUNTY ATTORNEY. I guess before we're through she may have something more serious than preserves to worry about.

HALE. Well, women are used to worrying over trifles.

(*The two women move a little closer together.*)

COUNTY ATTORNEY (*with the gallantry of a young politician*). And yet, for all their worries, what would we do without the ladies? (*The women do not unbend. He goes to the sink, takes a dipperful of water from the pail and pouring it into a basin, washes his hands. Starts to wipe them on the roller towel, turns it for a cleaner place.*) Dirty towels! (*Kicks his foot against the pans under the sink*) Not much of a housekeeper, would you say, ladies?

MRS. HALE (*stiffly*). There's a great deal of work to be done on a farm.

COUNTY ATTORNEY. To be sure. And yet (*with a little bow to her*) I know there are some Dickson county farmhouses which do not have such roller towels. (*He gives it a pull to expose its full length again.*)

MRS. HALE. Those towels get dirty awfully quick. Men's hands aren't always as clean as they might be.

COUNTY ATTORNEY. Ah, loyal to your sex, I see. But you and Mrs. Wright were neighbors. I suppose you were friends, too.

MRS. HALE (*shaking her head*). I've not seen much of her of late years. I've not been in this house—it's more than a year.

COUNTY ATTORNEY. And why was that? You didn't like her?

MRS. HALE. I liked her all well enough. Farmers' wives have their hands full, Mr. Henderson. And then—

COUNTY ATTORNEY. Yes—?

MRS. HALE (*looking about*). It never seemed a very cheerful place.

COUNTY ATTORNEY. No—It's not cheerful. I shouldn't say she had the homemaking instinct.

MRS. HALE. Well, I don't know as Wright had, either.

COUNTY ATTORNEY. You mean that they didn't get on very well?

MRS. HALE. No, I don't mean anything. But I don't think a place'd be any cheerfuller for John Wright's being in it.

COUNTY ATTORNEY. I'd like to talk more of that a little later. I want to get the lay of things upstairs now. (*He goes to the left, where three steps lead to a stair door.*)

SHERIFF. I suppose anything Mrs. Peters does'll be all right. She was to take in some clothes for her, you know, and a few little things. We left in such a hurry yesterday.

COUNTY ATTORNEY. Yes, but I would like to see what you take, Mrs. Peters, and keep an eye out for anything that might be of use to us.

MRS. PETERS. Yes, Mr. Henderson.

(*The women listen to the men's steps on the stairs, then look about the kitchen.*)

MRS. HALE. I'd hate to have men coming into my kitchen, snooping around and criticizing. (*She arranges the pans under sink which the* COUNTY ATTORNEY *had shoved out of place.*)

MRS. PETERS. Of course it's no more than their duty.

MRS. HALE. Duty's all right, but I guess that deputy sheriff that came out to make the fire might have got a little of this on. (*Gives the roller towel a pull*) Wish I'd thought of that sooner. Seems mean to talk about her for not having things slicked up when she had to come away in such a hurry.

MRS. PETERS (*who has gone to a small table in the left rear corner of the room, and lifted one end of a towel that covers a pan*). She had bread set. (*Stands still*)

MRS. HALE (*eyes fixed on a loaf of bread beside the breadbox, which is on a low shelf at the other side of the room. Moves slowly toward it*). She was going to put this in there. (*Picks up loaf, then abruptly drops it. In a manner of returning to familiar things*) It's a shame about her fruit. I wonder if it's all gone. (*Gets up on the chair and looks*) I think there's some here that's all right, Mrs. Peters. Yes—here; (*holding it toward the window*) this is cherries, too. (*Looking again*) I declare I believe that's the only one. (*Gets down, bottle in her hand. Goes to the sink and wipes it off on the outside*) She'll feel awful bad after all her hard work in the hot weather. I remember the afternoon I put up my cherries last summer.

(*She puts the bottle on the big kitchen table, center of the room. With a sigh, is about to sit down in the rocking chair. Before she is seated realizes what chair it is; with a slow look at it, steps back. The chair which she has touched rocks back and forth.*)

MRS. PETERS. Well, I must get those things from the front room closet. (*She goes to the door at the right, but after looking into the other room, steps back.*) You coming with me, Mrs. Hale? You could help me carry them.

(*They go in the other room; reappear,* MRS. PETERS *carrying a dress and skirt,* MRS. HALE *following with a pair of shoes.*)

MRS. PETERS. My, it's cold in there. (*She puts the clothes on the big table, and hurries to the stove.*)

MRS. HALE (*examining the skirt*). Wright was close. I think maybe that's why she kept so much to herself. She didn't even belong to the Ladies' Aid. I suppose she felt she couldn't do her part, and then you don't enjoy things when you feel shabby. She used to wear pretty clothes and be lively, when she was Minnie Foster, one of the town girls singing in the choir. But that—oh, that was thirty years ago. This all you was to take in?

MRS. PETERS. She said she wanted an apron. Funny thing to want, for there isn't much to get you dirty in jail, goodness knows. But I suppose just to make her feel more natural. She said they was in the top drawer in this cupboard. Yes, here. And then her little shawl that always hung behind the door. (*Opens stair door and looks*) Yes, here it is. (*Quickly shuts door leading upstairs*)

MRS. HALE (*abruptly moving toward her*). Mrs. Peters?

MRS. PETERS. Yes, Mrs. Hale?

MRS. HALE. Do you think she did it?

MRS. PETERS (*in a frightened voice*). Oh, I don't know.

MRS. HALE. Well, I don't think she did. Asking for an

apron and her little shawl. Worrying about her fruit.

MRS. PETERS (*starts to speak, glances up, where footsteps are heard in the room above. In a low voice*). Mr. Peters says it looks bad for her. Mr. Henderson is awful sarcastic in a speech and he'll make fun of her sayin' she didn't wake up.

MRS. HALE. Well, I guess John Wright didn't wake when they was slipping that rope under his neck.

MRS. PETERS. No, it's strange. It must have been done awful crafty and still. They say it was such a—funny way to kill a man, rigging it all up like that.

MRS. HALE. That's just what Mr. Hale said. There was a gun in the house. He says that's what he can't understand.

MRS. PETERS. Mr. Henderson said coming out that what was needed for the case was a motive; something to show anger, or—sudden feeling.

MRS. HALE (*who is standing by the table*). Well, I don't see any signs of anger around here. (*She puts her hand on the dish towel which lies on the table, stands looking down at table, one half of which is clean, the other half messy.*) It's wiped to here. (*Makes a move as if to finish work, then turns and looks at loaf of bread outside the breadbox. Drops towel. In that voice of coming back to familiar things*) Wonder how they are finding things upstairs. (*Crossing below table to downstage right*) I hope she had it a little more redd-up[2] up there. You know, it seems kind of *sneaking*. Locking her up in town and then coming out here and trying to get her own house to turn against her!

MRS. PETERS. But, Mrs. Hale, the law is the law.

MRS. HALE. I s'pose 'tis. (*Unbuttoning her coat*) Better loosen up your things, Mrs. Peters. You

---

[2] **redd-up:** put in order

won't feel them when you go out.

(MRS. PETERS *takes off her fur tippet, goes to hang it on hook at back of room, stands looking at the work basket on the floor near window.*)

MRS. PETERS. She was piecing a quilt.

(*She brings the large sewing basket to the center table and they look at the bright pieces.*)

MRS. HALE. It's a log-cabin pattern. Pretty, isn't it? I wonder if she was goin' to quilt it or just knot it?

(*Footsteps have been heard coming down the stairs. The* SHERIFF *enters followed by* HALE *and the* COUNTY ATTORNEY.)

SHERIFF. They wonder if she was going to quilt it or just knot it?

(*The men laugh, the women look abashed.*)

COUNTY ATTORNEY (*rubbing his hands over the stove*). Frank's fire didn't do much up there, did it? Well, let's go out to the barn and get that cleared up.

(*The men go outside.*)

MRS. HALE (*resentfully*). I don't know as there's anything so strange, our takin' up our time with little things while we're waiting for them to get the evidence. (*She sits down at the big table smoothing out a block with decision.*) I don't see as it's anything to laugh about.

MRS. PETERS (*apologetically*). Of course they've got awful important things on their minds. (*Pulls up a chair and joins* MRS. HALE *at the table*)

MRS. HALE (*examining another block*). Mrs. Peters, look at this one. Here, this is the one she was working on, and look at the sewing! All the rest of it has been so nice and even. And look at this! It's all over the place! Why, it looks as if she didn't know what she was about!

(*After she has said this they look at each other, then start to glance back at the door. After an instant* MRS. HALE *has pulled at a knot and ripped the sewing.*)

MRS. PETERS. Oh, what are you doing, Mrs. Hale?

MRS. HALE (*mildly*). Just pulling out a stitch or two that's not sewed very good. (*Threading a needle*) Bad sewing always made me fidgety.

MRS. PETERS (*nervously*). I don't think we ought to touch things.

MRS. HALE. I'll just finish up this end. (*Suddenly stopping and leaning forward*) Mrs. Peters?

MRS. PETERS. Yes, Mrs. Hale?

MRS. HALE. What do you suppose she was so nervous about?

MRS. PETERS. Oh—I don't know. I don't know as she was nervous. I sometimes sew awful queer when I'm just tired. (MRS. HALE *starts to say something, looks at* MRS. PETERS, *then goes on sewing.*) Well, I must get these things wrapped up. They may be through sooner than we think. (*putting apron and other things together*) I wonder where I can find a piece of paper, and string.

MRS. HALE. In that cupboard, maybe.

MRS. PETERS (*looking in cupboard*). Why, here's a bird-cage. (*Holds it up*) Did she have a bird, Mrs. Hale?

MRS. HALE. Why, I don't know whether she did or not—

I've not been here for so long. There was a man around last year selling canaries cheap, but I don't know as she took one; maybe she did. She used to sing real pretty herself.

MRS. PETERS (*glancing around*). Seems funny to think of a bird here. But she must have had one, or why would she have a cage? I wonder what happened to it?

MRS. HALE. I s'pose maybe the cat got it.

MRS. PETERS. No, she didn't have a cat. She's got that feeling some people have about cats—being afraid of them. My cat got in her room and she was real upset and asked me to take it out.

MRS. HALE. My sister Bessie was like that. Queer ain't it?

MRS. PETERS (*examining the cage*). Why, look at this door. It's broke. One hinge is pulled apart.

MRS. HALE (*looking too*). Looks as if someone must have been rough with it.

MRS. PETERS. Why, yes. (*She brings the cage forward and puts it on the table.*)

MRS. HALE. I wish if they're going to find any evidence they'd be about it. I don't like this place.

MRS. PETERS. But I'm awful glad you came with me, Mrs. Hale. It would be lonesome for me sitting here alone.

MRS. HALE. It would, wouldn't it? (*Dropping her sewing*) But I tell you what I do wish, Mrs. Peters. I wish I had come over sometimes when *she* was here. I—(*looking around the room*)—wish I had.

MRS. PETERS. But of course you were awful busy, Mrs. Hale—your house and your children.

MRS. HALE. I could've come. I stayed away because it weren't cheerful—and that's why I ought to have come. I—I've never liked this place. Maybe because it's down in a hollow and you don't see the road. I dunno what it is, but it's a lonesome place and always was. I wish I had come over to see Minnie Foster sometimes. I can see now—(*Shakes her head*)

MRS. PETERS. Well, you mustn't reproach yourself, Mrs. Hale. Somehow we just don't see how it is with other folks until—something turns up.

MRS. HALE. Not having children makes less work—but it makes a quiet house, and Wright out to work all day, and no company when he did come in. Did you know John Wright, Mrs. Peters?

MRS. PETERS. Not to know him; I've seen him in town. They say he was a good man.

MRS. HALE. Yes—good; he didn't drink, and kept his word as well as most, I guess, and paid his debts. But he was a hard man, Mrs. Peters. Just to pass the time of day with him—(*Shivers*) Like a raw wind that gets to the bone. (*Pauses, her eye falling on the cage*) I should think she would 'a' wanted a bird. But what do you suppose went with it?

MRS. PETERS. I don't know, unless it got sick and died.

(*She reaches over and swings the broken door, swings it again, both women watch it.*)

MRS. HALE. You weren't raised round here, were you? (MRS. PETERS *shakes her head.*) You didn't know—her?

MRS. PETERS. Not till they brought her yesterday.

MRS. HALE. She—come to think of it, she was kind of like a bird herself—real sweet and pretty, but kind of timid and—fluttery. How—she—did—change. (*Silence; then as if struck by a happy thought and relieved to get back to everyday things.*) Tell you what, Mrs. Peters, why don't you take the quilt in with you? It might take up her mind.

MRS. PETERS. Why, I think that's a real nice idea, Mrs. Hale. There couldn't possibly be any objection to it, could there? Now, just what would I take? I wonder if her patches are in here—and her things.

(*They look in the sewing basket.*)

MRS. HALE. Here's some red. I expect this has got sewing things in it. (*Brings out a fancy box*) What a pretty box. Looks like something somebody would give you. Maybe her scissors are in here. (*Opens box. Suddenly puts her hand to her nose*) Why—(MRS. PETERS *bends nearer, then turns her face away.*) There's something wrapped up in this piece of silk.
MRS. PETERS. Why, this isn't her scissors.
MRS. HALE. (*lifting the silk*). Oh, Mrs. Peters—it's—

(MRS. PETERS *bends closer.*)

MRS. PETERS. It's the bird.
MRS. HALE (*jumping up*). But, Mrs. Peters—look at it! Its neck! Look at its neck! It's all—other side *to*.
MRS. PETERS. Somebody—wrung—its—neck.

(*Their eyes meet. A look of growing comprehension, of horror. Steps are heard outside.* MRS. HALE *slips box under quilt pieces, and sinks into her chair. Enter* SHERIFF *and* COUNTY ATTORNEY. MRS. PETERS *rises.*)

COUNTY ATTORNEY (*as one turning from serious things to little pleasantries*). Well, ladies, have you decided whether she was going to quilt it or knot it?
MRS. PETERS. We think she was going to—knot it.
COUNTY ATTORNEY. Well, that's interesting, I'm sure.

(*Seeing the birdcage*) Has the bird flown?

MRS. HALE (*putting more quilt pieces over the box*). We think the—cat got it.

COUNTY ATTORNEY (*preoccupied*). Is there a cat?

(MRS. HALE *glances in a quick covert way at* MRS. PETERS.)

MRS. PETERS. Well, not *now*. They're superstitious, you know. They leave.

COUNTY ATTORNEY (*to* SHERIFF PETERS, *continuing an interrupted conversation*). No sign at all of anyone having come from the outside. Their own rope. Now let's go up again and go over it piece by piece. (*They start upstairs.*) It would have to have been someone who knew just the—

(MRS. PETERS *sits down. The two women sit there not looking at one another, but as if peering into something and at the same time holding back. When they talk now it is in the manner of feeling their way over strange ground, as if afraid of what they are saying, but as if they cannot help saying it.*)

MRS. HALE. She liked the bird. She was going to bury it in that pretty box.

MRS. PETERS (*in a whisper*). When I was a girl—my kitten—there was a boy took a hatchet, and before my eyes—and before I could get there—(*covers her face an instant*) If they hadn't held me back I would have (*catches herself, looks upstairs where steps are heard, falters weakly*)—hurt him.

MRS. HALE (*with a slow look around her*). I wonder how it would seem never to have had any children around.

(*Pause*) No, Wright wouldn't like the bird—a thing that sang. She used to sing. He killed that, too.

MRS. PETERS (*moving uneasily*). We don't know who killed the bird.

MRS. HALE. I knew John Wright.

MRS. PETERS. It was an awful thing was done in this house that night, Mrs. Hale. Killing a man while he slept, slipping a rope around his neck that choked the life out of him.

MRS. HALE. His neck. Choked the life out of him. (*Her hand goes out and rests on the birdcage.*)

MRS. PETERS (*with rising voice*). We don't know who killed him. We don't know.

MRS. HALE (*her own feeling not interrupted*). If there'd been years and years of nothing, then a bird to sing to you, it would be awful—still, after the bird was still.

MRS. PETERS (*something within her speaking*). I know what stillness is. When we homesteaded in Dakota, and my first baby died—after he was two years old, and me with no other then—

MRS. HALE (*moving*). How soon do you suppose they'll be through looking for the evidence?

MRS. PETERS. I know what stillness is. (*Pulling herself back*) The law has got to punish crime, Mrs. Hale.

MRS. HALE (*not as if answering that*). I wish you'd seen Minnie Foster when she wore a white dress with blue ribbons and stood up there in the choir and sang. (*A look around the room*) Oh, I *wish* I'd come over here once in a while! That was a crime! That was a crime! Who's going to punish that?

MRS. PETERS (*looking upstairs*). We mustn't—take on.

MRS. HALE. I might have known she needed help! I know how things can be—for women. I tell you, it's queer, Mrs. Peters. We live close together and we live far apart.

We all go through the same things—it's all just a different kind of the same thing. (*Brushes her eyes; noticing the bottle of fruit, reaches out for it*) If I was you I wouldn't tell her her fruit was gone. Tell her it *ain't*. Tell her it's all right. Take this in to prove it to her. She—she may never know whether it was broke or not.

MRS. PETERS (*takes the bottle, looks about for something to wrap it in; takes petticoat from the clothes brought from the other room, very nervously begins winding this around the bottle. In a false voice*). My, it's a good thing the men couldn't hear us. Wouldn't they just laugh! Getting all stirred up over a little thing like a—dead canary. As if that could have anything to do with—with—wouldn't they *laugh*!

(*The men are heard coming downstairs.*)

MRS. HALE (*under her breath*). Maybe they would—maybe they wouldn't.

COUNTY ATTORNEY. No, Peters, it's all perfectly clear except a reason for doing it. But you know juries when it comes to women. If there was some definite thing. Something to show—something to make a story about—a thing that would connect up with this strange way of doing it—

(*The women's eyes meet for an instant. Enter* HALE *from outer door.*)

HALE. Well, I've got the team around. Pretty cold out there.

COUNTY ATTORNEY. I'm going to stay here awhile by myself. (*To the* SHERIFF) You can send Frank out for me, can't you? I want to go over everything. I'm not satisfied that we can't do better.

SHERIFF. Do you want to see what Mrs. Peters is going to take in?

(*The* COUNTY ATTORNEY *goes to the table, picks up the apron, laughs.*)

COUNTY ATTORNEY. Oh, I guess they're not very dangerous things the ladies have picked out. (*Moves a few things about, disturbing the quilt pieces which cover the box. Steps back*) No, Mrs. Peters doesn't need supervising. For that matter, a sheriff's wife is married to the law. Ever think of it that way, Mrs. Peters?

MRS. PETERS. Not—just that way.

SHERIFF (*chuckling*). Married to the law. (*Moves toward the other room*) I just want you to come in here a minute, George. We ought to take a look at these windows.

COUNTY ATTORNEY (*scoffingly*). Oh, windows!

SHERIFF. We'll be right out, Mr. Hale.

(HALE *goes outside. The* SHERIFF *follows the* COUNTY ATTORNEY *into the other room. Then* MRS. HALE *rises, hands tight together, looking intensely at* MRS. PETERS, *whose eyes make a slow turn, finally meeting* MRS. HALE'S. *A moment* MRS. HALE *holds her, then her own eyes point the way to where the box is concealed. Suddenly* MRS. PETERS *throws back quilt pieces and tries to put the box in the bag she is carrying. It is too big. She opens box, starts to take bird out, cannot touch it, goes to pieces, stands there helpless. Sound of a knob turning in the other room.* MRS. HALE *snatches the box and puts it in the pocket of her big coat. Enter* COUNTY ATTORNEY *and* SHERIFF.)

COUNTY ATTORNEY (*facetiously*). Well, Henry, at least we

found out that she was not going to quilt it. She was going to—what is it you call it, ladies?

MRS. HALE (*her hands against her pocket*). We call it—knot it, Mr. Henderson.

CURTAIN

A Wish Named Arnold

Charles de Lint

Marguerite kept a wish in a brass egg, and its name was Arnold.

The egg screwed apart in the middle. Inside, wrapped in a small piece of faded velvet, was the wish. It was a small wish, about the length of a man's thumb, and was made of black clay in the rough shape of a bird. Marguerite decided straight away that it was a crow, even if it did have a splash of white on its head. That made it just more special for her, because she'd dyed a forelock of her own dark hair a peroxide white just before the summer started—much to her parents' dismay.

She'd found the egg under a pile of junk in Miller's while tagging along with her mother and aunt on their usual weekend tour of the local antique shops. Miller's was near their cottage on Otty Lake, just down the road from Rideau Ferry, and considered to be the best antique shop in the area.

The egg and its dubious contents were only two dollars, and maybe the egg was dinged up a little and didn't screw together quite right, and maybe the carving didn't look so much like a crow as it did a lump of black clay with what could be a beak on it, but she'd bought it all the same.

It wasn't until Arnold talked to her that she found out he was a wish.

"What do you mean, you're a wish?" she'd asked, keeping her voice low so that her parents wouldn't think she'd taken to talking in her sleep. "Like a genie in a lamp?"

Something like that.

It was all quite confusing. Arnold lay in her hand, an unmoving lump that was definitely not alive even if he did look like a bird, sort of. That was a plain fact, as her father liked to say. On the other hand, someone was definitely speaking to her in a low, buzzing voice that tickled pleasantly inside her head.

I wonder if I'm dreaming, she thought.

She gave her white forelock a tug, then brushed it away from her brow and bent down to give the clay bird a closer look.

"What sort of a wish can you give me?" she asked finally.

Think of something—any one thing that you want—and I'll give it to you.

"Anything?"

Within reasonable limits.

Marguerite nodded sagely. She was all too familiar with *that* expression. "Reasonable limits" was why she only had one forelock dyed instead of a whole swath of rainbow colors like her friend Tina, or a Mohawk like Sheila. If she just washed her hair and let it dry, *and* you ignored the dyed forelock, she had a most reasonable short haircut. But all it took was a little gel that she kept hidden in her purse, and by the time she joined her friends down at the mall, her hair was sticking out around her head in a bristle of spikes. It was just such a pain wearing a hat when she came home and having to wash out the gel right away.

Maybe that should be her wish. That she could go around looking just however she pleased and nobody could tell her any different. Except that seemed like a waste of a wish. She should probably ask for great heaps of money and jewels. Or maybe for a hundred more wishes.

"How come I only get one wish?" she asked.

Because that's all I am, Arnold replied. *One small wish.*

"Genies and magic fish give three. In fact, *everybody* in *all* the stories gets three. Isn't it a tradition or some-thing?"

Not where I come from.

"Where *do* you come from?"

There was a moment's pause, then Arnold said softly, *I'm not really sure.*

Marguerite felt a little uncomfortable at that. The voice tickling her mind sounded too sad, and she started to feel ashamed of being so greedy.

"Listen," she said. "I didn't really mean to . . . you know. . ."

That's all right, Arnold replied. *Just let me know when you've decided what your wish is.*

Marguerite got a feeling in her head as though some-thing had just slipped away, like a lost memory or a half-remembered thought; then she realized that Arnold had just gone back to wherever it was that he'd been before she'd opened the egg. Thoughtfully she wrapped him up in the faded velvet, then shut him away in the egg. She put the egg under her pillow and went to sleep.

All the next day she kept thinking about the brass egg and the clay crow inside it, about her one wish and all the wonderful things that there were to wish for. She meant to take out the egg right away, first thing in the morning, but she never quite found the time. She went fishing with her father after breakfast, and then she went into Perth to shop with her mother, and then she went swimming with Steve, who lived two cottages down and liked punk music as much as she did, though maybe for different reasons. She didn't get back to her egg until bedtime that night.

"What happens to you after I've made my wish?" she asked after she'd taken Arnold out of his egg.

I go away.

Marguerite asked, "Where to?" before she really thought about what she was saying, but this time Arnold didn't get upset.

To be somebody else's wish, he said.

"And after that?"

Well, after they've made their wish, I'll go on to the next, and the next . . .

"It sounds kind of boring."

Oh, no. I get to meet all sorts of interesting people.

Marguerite scratched her nose. She'd gotten a mosquito bite right on the end of it and felt very much like Pinocchio, though she hadn't been telling any lies.

"Have you always been a wish?" she asked, not thinking again.

Arnold's voice grew so quiet that it was just a feathery touch in her mind. *I remember being something else . . . a long time ago. . . .*

Marguerite leaned closer, as though that would help her hear him better. But there was a sudden feeling in her as though Arnold had shaken himself out of his reverie.

Do you know what you're going to wish for yet? he asked briskly.

"Not exactly."

Well, just let me know when you're ready, he said, and then he was gone again.

Marguerite sighed and put him away. This didn't seem to be at all the way this whole wishing business should go. Instead of feeling all excited about being able to ask for any one thing—*anything!*—she felt guilty because she kept making Arnold feel bad. Mind you, she thought . . . . He did seem to be a gloomy sort of a genie when you came right down to it.

She fell asleep wondering if he looked the same in whatever place he went to when he left her as he did when she held him in her hand. Somehow his ticklish, raspy voice didn't quite go with the lumpy clay figure that lay inside the brass egg. She supposed she'd never know.

As the summer progressed they became quite good friends, in an odd sort of way. Marguerite took to carrying the egg around with her in a small, quilted, cotton bag that she slung over her shoulder. At opportune moments, she'd take Arnold out and they'd talk about all sorts of things.

Arnold, Marguerite discovered, knew a lot that she hadn't supposed a genie would know. He was up on all the latest bands, seemed to have seen all the best movies, knew stories that could make her giggle uncontrollably or shiver with chills under her blankets late at night. If she didn't press him for information about his past, he proved to be the best friend a person could want, and she found herself telling him things that she'd never think of telling anyone else.

It got to the point where Marguerite forgot he was a wish. Which was fine until the day she left her quilted cotton bag behind in a restaurant in Smith Falls on a day's outing with her mother. She became totally panic-stricken until her mother took her back to the restaurant, but by then her bag was gone, and so was the egg, and with it, Arnold.

Marguerite was inconsolable. She moped around for days, and nothing that anyone could do could cheer her up. She missed Arnold passionately. Missed their long talks when she was supposed to be sleeping. Missed the weight of his egg in her shoulder bag and the companionable presence of just knowing he was there. And also, she realized, she'd missed her chance of using her wish.

She could have had anything she wanted. She could have asked for piles of money. For fame and fortune. To be a lead singer in a band like "10,000 Maniacs." To be another Molly Ringwald and star in all kinds of movies. She could have wished that Arnold would stay with her forever. Instead, jerk that she was, she'd never used the wish, and now she had nothing. How could she be so stupid?

"Oh," she muttered one night in her bed. "I wish I . . . I wish . . ."

She paused then, feeling a familiar tickle in her head.

Did you finally decide on your wish? Arnold asked.

Marguerite sat up so suddenly that she knocked over her water glass on the night table. Luckily it was empty.

"Arnold?" she asked, looking around. "Are you here?"

Well, not exactly here, as it were, but I can hear you.

"Where have you *been*?"

Waiting for you to make your wish.

"I've really missed you," Marguerite said. She patted her comforter with eager hands, trying to find Arnold's egg. "How did you get back here?"

I'm not exactly here, Arnold said.

"How come you never talked to me, when I've been

missing you all this time?"

I can't really initiate these things, Arnold explained. *It gets rather complicated, but even though my egg's with someone else, I can't really be their wish until I've finished being yours.*

"So we can still talk and be friends even though I've lost the egg?"

Not exactly. I can fulfill your wish, but since I'm not with you, as it were, I can't really stay unless you're ready to make your wish.

"You can't?" Marguerite wailed.

Afraid not. I don't make the rules, you know.

"I've got it," Marguerite said. And she did have it, too. If she wanted to keep Arnold with her, all she had to do was wish for him to always be her friend. Then no one could take him away from her. They'd always be together.

"I wish . . ." she began.

But that didn't seem quite right, she realized. She gave her dyed forelock a nervous tug. It wasn't right to *make* someone be your friend. But if she didn't do that, if she wished something else, then Arnold would just go off and be somebody else's wish. Oh, if only things didn't have to be complicated. Maybe she should just wish herself to the moon and be done with all her problems. She could lie there and stare at the world from a nice, long distance away while she slowly asphyxiated. That would solve everything.

She felt that telltale feeling in her mind that let her know that Arnold was leaving again.

"Wait," she said. "I haven't made my wish yet."

The feeling stopped. *Then you've decided?* Arnold asked.

She hadn't, but as soon as he asked, she realized that there was only one fair wish she could make.

"I wish you were free," she said.

The feeling that was Arnold moved blurrily inside her. *You what?* he asked.

"I wish you were free. I *can* wish that, can't I?"

Yes, but . . . wouldn't you rather have something . . . well, something for yourself?

"This *is* for myself," Marguerite said. "Your being free would be the best thing I could wish for, because you're my friend and I don't want you to be trapped any-more." She paused for a moment, brow wrinkling. "Or is there a rule against that?"

No rule, Arnold said softly. His ticklish voice bubbled with excitement. *No rule at all against it.*

"Then that's my wish," Marguerite said.

Inside her mind, she felt a sensation like a tiny whirl-wind spinning around and around. It was like Arnold's voice and an autumn-leaves smell and a kaleidoscope of dervishing lights, all wrapped up in one whirling sensation.

Free! Arnold called from the center of that whirlygig. *Free free free!*

A sudden weight was in Marguerite's hand, and she saw that the brass egg had appeared there. It lay open on her palm, the faded velvet spilled out of it. It seemed so very small to hold so much happiness, but fluttering on tiny wings was the clay crow, rising up in a spin that twinned Arnold's presence in Marguerite's mind.

Her fingers closed around the brass egg as Arnold doubled, then tripled his size, in an explosion of black feathers. His voice was like a chorus of bells, ringing and ringing between Marguerite's ears. Then with an exuber-ant caw, he stroked the air with his wings, flew out the cottage window, and was gone.

Marguerite sat quietly, staring out the window and holding the brass egg. A big grin stretched her lips. There was something so *right* about what she'd just done that she felt an overwhelming sense of happiness herself, as though she'd been the one trapped in a treadmill of wishes in a brass egg and Arnold had been the one to free *her*.

At last she reached out and picked up from the comforter a small, glossy, black feather that Arnold had left behind. Wrapping it in the old velvet, she put it into the brass egg and screwed the egg shut once more.

That September a new family moved in next door with a boy her age named Arnold. Marguerite was delighted, and though her parents were surprised, she and the new boy became best friends almost immediately. She showed him the egg one day that winter and wasn't at all surprised that the feather she still kept in it was the exact same shade of black as her new friend's hair.

Arnold stroked the feather with one finger when she let him see it. He smiled at her and said, "I had a wish once. . . ."

the
YELLOW
BALL

Phillipa Pearce

The ladder reached comfortably to the branch of the sycamore they had decided on; and its foot was held steady by Lizzie, while her father climbed up. He carried the rope—nylon, for strength—in loops over his shoulder. He knotted one end securely round the chosen branch, and then let the other end drop. It fell to dangle only a little to one side of where Con held the old car-tyre upright on the ground. Really, of course, there was no need for the tyre to be held in that position yet; but something had to be found for Con to do, to take his mind off the cows in the meadow. He was nervous of animals, and cows were large.

Their father prepared to descend the ladder.

And then—how exactly did it happen? Why did it happen? Was Con really the first to notice the knot-hole in the tree-trunk, as he later claimed? Or did Lizzie point it out? Would their father, anyway, have reached over sideways from the ladder—as he now did—to dip his fingers into the cavity?

"There's something in here . . . something stuck . . ." He teetered a little on the ladder as he tugged. "Got it!"

And, as he grasped whatever was in the hole, the air round the group in the meadow tightened, tautened with expectancy.

Something was going to happen . . .

Going to happen . . .

To happen . . .

"Here we are!" He was holding aloft a dingy, spherical object. "A ball . . . it's a ball! A chance in a thousand; someone threw a ball high, and it happened to lodge here! No, a chance in a million for it to have happened like that!"

He dropped the ball. Lizzie tried to catch it, but was prevented by the ladder. Con tried, but was prevented by the tyre he held. The ball bounced, but not high, rolled out a little way over the meadow, came to rest.

And something invisibly in the meadow breathed again, watchful, but relaxed . . .

The two children forgot the ball, because their father was now down from the ladder; he was knotting the free end of the rope round the tyre, so that it cleared the ground by about half a metre. It hung there, enticingly.

While their father put his ladder away, the children began arguing about who should have first go on the tyre. He came back, sharply stopped their quarrelling, and showed them how both could get on at the same time: they must face each other, with both pairs of legs through the circle of the tyre, but in opposite directions. So they sat on the lowest curve of the tyre, gripping the rope from which it hung; and their father began to swing them, higher and higher, wider and wider.

As they swung up, the setting sun was in their eyes, and suddenly they saw the whole of the meadow, but tilted, tipped; and they saw the houses on the other side of the meadow rushing towards them; and then as they swung back again, the houses were rushing away, and the meadow too—

Swinging—swinging—they whooped and shrieked for joy.

Their mother came out to watch for a little, and then said they must all come in for tea. So all three went in, through the little gate from the meadow into the garden, and then into the house. They left the tyre still swaying; they left the dirty old ball where it had rolled and come to rest and been forgotten.

As soon as he had finished his tea, Con was eager to be in the meadow, to have the tyre to himself while there was still daylight. Lizzie went on munching.

But, in a few moments, he was indoors again, saying hesitantly: "I think—I think there's someone in the meadow waiting for me."

Their father said: "Nonsense, boy! The cows will never hurt you!"

"It's not the cows at all. There's someone waiting. For me."

Their mother looked at their father: "Perhaps . . . "

"I'll come out with you," he said to Con; and so he did; and Lizzie followed them both.

But Con was saying: "I didn't say I was afraid. I just said there was someone in the meadow. I thought there was. That's all." They went through the garden gate into the meadow. "Man or woman?" Con's father asked him. "Or boy or girl?"

"No," said Con. "It wasn't like that."

His father had scanned the wide meadow thoroughly.

"No one at all." He sighed. "Oh, Conrad, your *imagination!* I'm going back before the tea's too cold. You two can stay a bit longer, if you like. Till it begins to get dark."

He went indoors.

Lizzie, looking beyond the tyre, and remembering after all, said: "That ball's gone."

"I picked it up." Con brought it out of his pocket, held it out to Lizzie. She took it. It was smaller than a tennis-ball, but heavier, because solid. One could see that it was yellow under the dirtiness—and it was not really so very dirty after all. Dirt had collected in the tiny, shallow holes with which the surface of the ball was pitted. That was all.

"I wonder what made the holes," said Lizzie.

Con held out his hand for the ball again. Lizzie did not give up: "It's just as much mine as yours." They glared at each other, but uneasily. They did not really *want* to quarrel about this ball; this ball was for better things than that.

"I suppose we could take turns at having it," said Lizzie. "Or perhaps you don't really want the ball, Con?"

"But I do—I do!" At the second "do" he lunged forward, snatched the ball from his sister and was through the gate with it, back towards the house—and Lizzie was after him. The gate clicked shut behind them both—

Suddenly they both stopped, and turned to look back. Oh! they knew that something was coming—

High, and over—

They saw it—or rather, they *had* seen it, for it happened so swiftly—

A small, dark shape, a shadow had leapt the shut gate after them—elegant as a dancer in flying motion—eager—

Con breathed: "Did you see him?"

"Her," Lizzie whispered back. "A bitch. I saw the teats, as she came over the gate."

"Her ears lifted in the wind . . . "

"She had her eyes on the ball—oh, Con! It's *her* ball! Hers! She wants it—she wants it!"

Though nothing was visible now, they could feel the air of the garden quivering with hope and expectancy.

"Throw it for her, Con!" Lizzie urged him. "Throw it!"

With all his strength, Con threw the yellow ball over the gate and out into the meadow, and the shadow of a shape followed it in another noble leap and then a long darting movement across the meadow, straight as an arrow after the ball, seeming to gain on it, to be about to catch up with it, to catch it—

But when the ball came to rest, the other movement still went on, not in a straight line any more, but sweeping to and fro, quartering the ground, seeking—seeking—

"It's her ball: why doesn't she find it and pick it up?" Con asked wonderingly. "It's there for her."

Lizzie said: "I think—I think it's because it's a real ball, and she's not a real dog. She can't pick it up, poor thing: she's only some kind of ghost."

A ghost! Con said nothing, but drew closer to his sister. They stood together in the garden, looking out into the meadow, while they accustomed their minds to what they were seeing. They stood on the solid earth of the garden-path; behind them was their house, with the lights now on and their father drinking his cups of tea; in front of them lay the meadow with the sycamore tree; in the far distance, the cows.

All real, all solid, all familiar.

And in the middle of the meadow—to and fro, to and fro—moved the ghost of a dog.

But now Con moved away from his sister, stood

stalwartly alone again. An ordinary ghost might have frightened him for longer; a real dog would certainly have frightened him. But the ghost of a dog—that was different!

"Lizzie," he said, "let's not tell anyone. Not anyone. It's our private ghost. Just ours."

"All right."

They continued gazing over the meadow until they could see no longer through the deepening dusk. Then their mother was rapping on the window for them to come indoors, and they had to go.

Indoors, their parents asked them: "Did you have a good swing on the tyre?"

"The tyre?" They stared, and said: "We forgot."

Later, they went into the meadow again with a torch to look for the yellow ball. They were on the alert, but there was now nobody, nothing that was waiting—even when Con, holding the ball in his hand, pretended that he was about to throw it. No ardent expectation. Nothing now but the meadow and the trees in it and the unsurprised cows.

They brought the ball indoors and scrubbed it as clean as they could with a nailbrush; but there would always be dirt in the little holes. "Those are toothmarks," said Con.

"Hers," said Lizzie. "This was her own special ball that she used to carry in her mouth when she was alive, when she was a flesh-and-blood dog."

"Where did she live?" asked Con. But, of course, Lizzie didn't know: perhaps in one of the houses by the meadow; perhaps even in their own, before ever they came to it.

"Shall we see her tomorrow?" asked Con. "Oh, I want to see her again tomorrow!"

The next day they took the yellow ball into the

meadow before school, but with no result. They tried again as soon as they got home: nothing. They had their tea and went out to the tyre again with the yellow ball. Nobody—nothing—was waiting for them. So they settled themselves on the tyre and swung to and fro, but gently, and talked to each other in low voices; and the sun began to set.

It was almost dusk, and they were still gently swinging, when Lizzie whispered: "She's here now—I'm sure of it!" Lizzie had been holding on to the nylon rope with one hand only, because the other held the yellow ball—it was her turn with it today, they had decided. Now she put her feet down to stop the swinging of the tyre, and stepped out from it altogether.

"Here, you!" she called softly; and, aside to Con, "Oh, I wish we knew her name!"

"Don't bother about that," said Con. "Throw the ball!"

So Lizzie did. They both saw where it went; also they glimpsed the flashing speed that followed it. And then began the fruitless searching, to and fro, to and fro . . .

"The poor thing!" said Lizzie, watching.

Con was only pleased and excited. He still sat on the tyre, and now he began to push hard with his toes, to swing higher and higher, chanting under his breath: "We've got a ghost—a ghooooost! We've got a ghost—a ghooooost!" Twice he stopped his swinging and chanting and left the tyre to fetch the ball and throw it again. (Lizzie did not want to throw it.) Each time they watched the straight following of the ball and then the spreading search that could not possibly have an end. But when darkness began to fall, they felt suddenly that there was no more ghost in the meadow; and it was time for them to go indoors, too.

As they went, Con said, almost shyly: "Tomorrow, when it's really my turn, do you think if I held the ball out to her and sort of *tempted* her with it, that she'd come close up to me? I might touch her . . ."

Lizzie said: "You can't touch a ghost. And besides, Con, you're frightened of dogs. You know you are. Else we might have had one of our own—a real one—years ago."

Con simply said: "This dog is different. I like this dog."

This first evening with the ghost-dog was only a beginning. Every day now they took the yellow ball into the meadow. They soon found that their ghost-dog came only at sunset, at dusk. Someone in the past had made a habit of giving this dog a ball-game in the evening, before going indoors for the night. A ball-game—that was all the dog hoped for. That was why she came at the end of the day, whenever a human hand held the yellow ball.

"And I think I can guess why Dad found the ball where he did, high up in a tree," said Lizzie. "It was put there deliberately, after the dog had died. Someone, probably the person who owned the dog—put it where no one was ever likely to find it. That someone wanted the ball not to be thrown again, because it was a haunted ball, you might say. It would draw the dog—the ghost of the dog—to come back to chase it and search for it and never find it. Never find it. Never."

"You make everything sound sad and wrong," said Con. "But it isn't, really."

Lizzie did not answer.

They had settled into a routine with their ghost-dog. They kept her yellow ball inside the hollow of the tyre, and brought it out every evening to throw it, in turns. Con always threw in his turn, but Lizzie often did not want to for hers. Then Con wanted to have her turn for himself, and at first she let him. Then she changed her mind: she insisted that, on her evenings, neither of them threw. Con was annoyed ("Dog-in-the-manger," he muttered), but, after all, Lizzie had the right.

A Saturday was coming when neither of them would throw, for a different reason. There was going to be a family expedition to the Zoo, in London; they were all going on a cheap day-excursion by train; and they would not be home until well after dark.

The day came, and the visit to the Zoo went as well as such visits do; and now at last they were on the train again, going home. All four were tired, but only their parents were dozing. Con was wide awake, and excited by the train. He pointed out to Lizzie that all the lights had come on inside the railway carriage; outside, the view was of dark landscapes and the sparkling illumination of towns, villages and highways.

The ticket-inspector came round, and Lizzie nudged their father awake. He found their four tickets, and they were clipped.

"And what about the dog?" said the ticket-inspector with severity.

"Dog?" Their father was still half-asleep, confused.

"Your dog. It should have a ticket. And why isn't it in the guard's van?"

"But there's no dog! We haven't a dog with us. We don't own a dog."

"I saw one," said the inspector grimly. He stooped and began looking under the seats; and other passengers began looking too, even while they all agreed that they had seen no dog.

And there really was no dog.

"Sorry, sir," said the ticket-inspector at last. His odd

mistake had shaken him. "I could have sworn I saw something move that was a dog." He took off his glasses and worried at the lenses with his handkerchief, and passed on.

The passengers resettled themselves; and when their own parents were dozing off again, Lizzie whispered to Con: "Con, you little demon! You brought it with you—the yellow ball!"

"Yes!" He held his pocket a little open and towards her, so that she saw the ball nestling inside. "And I had my hand on it, holding it, when the ticket-man came to us. And it worked! It worked! He was so pleased with himself that he was bouncing up and down in his seat.

Lizzie said in a furious whisper: "You should never have done it! Think how terrified that dog must have been to find herself on a train—a *train*! Con, how could you treat a dog so?"

"She was all right," Con said stubbornly. "She can't come to any harm, anyway: she's not a dog, she's only the ghost of one. And, anyway, it's as much my yellow ball as yours. We each have a half share in it."

"You never asked my permission about my half of the ball," said Lizzie, "and don't talk so loud, someone will hear."

They talked no more in so public a place, nor when they got home. They all went straight to bed, and all slept late the next morning, Sunday.

All except for Lizzie; she was up early, for her own purposes. She crept into Con's room, as he slept, and took the yellow ball from his pocket. She took it down the garden path to her father's work-shed, at the bottom. She and the yellow ball went inside, and Lizzie shut the door behind them.

Much later, when he was swinging on the tyre in the

morning sunshine, Con saw Lizzie coming into the meadow. He called to her: "All right! I know you've taken it, so there! You can have it today, anyway; but it's my turn tomorrow. We share the yellow ball. Remember?"

Lizzie came close to him. She held out towards him her right hand, closed; then she opened it carefully, palm upwards. "Yours," she said. On her flattened palm sat the domed shape of half the yellow ball. She twisted her hand slightly, so that the yellow dome fell on its side; then Con could see the sawn cross-section—black except for the outer rim of yellow.

For a moment Con was stunned. Then he screamed at her: "Wherever you hide your half, I'll find it! I'll glue the halves together! I'll make the yellow ball again and I'll throw it—I'll throw it and I'll throw it and I'll throw it!"

"No, you won't," said Lizzie. This time she held out towards him her cupped left hand: he saw a mess of chips and crumbs and granules of black, dotted with yellow. It had taken Lizzie a long time in her father's workshop to saw and cut and chip and grate her half-ball down to this. She said flatly: "I've destroyed the yellow ball for ever." Then, with a gesture of horror, she flung the ball particles from her and burst into a storm of sobbing and crying.

Only the shock of seeing Lizzie crying in such a way— she rarely cried at all—stopped Con from going for her with fists and feet and teeth as well. But the grief and desolation that he saw in Lizzie made him know his own affliction: grief at loss overwhelmed his first rage, and he began to cry, too.

"Why did you have to do that to the yellow ball, Lizzie? Why didn't you just hide it from me? Up a tree again: I might not have found it."

"Somebody would have found it, some day . . . "

"Or in the earth: you could have dug a deep hole, Lizzie."

"Somebody would have found it . . ."

"Oh, it wasn't fair of you, Lizzie!"

"No, it wasn't fair. But it was the only way. Otherwise she would search for ever for something she could never find."

"Go away," said Con.

Lizzie picked up the half-ball from the ground, where she had let it fall. She took it back with her to the house, to the dustbin. Then she went indoors and upstairs to her bedroom and lay down on her bed and cried again.

They kept apart all day, as far as possible; but, in the early evening, Lizzie saw Con on the tyre, and she went out to him, and he let her swing him gently to and fro. After a while he said: "We'll never see her again, shall we?"

"No," said Lizzie; "but at least she won't be worried and disappointed and unhappy again, either."

"I just miss her so," said Con. "If we can't have the ghost of a dog, I wish we had a real dog."

"But, Con—"

"No, truly, I wouldn't be frightened if we had a dog like her—just like her. It would have to be a bitch—she was black, wasn't she, Lizzie?"

"I thought so. A glossy black. I remember, her collar was red. Red against black: it looked smart."

"A glossy black bitch with a whippy tail and those big soft ears that flew out. That's what I'd like."

"Oh, Con!" cried Lizzie. She had always longed for them to have a dog; and it had never been possible because of Con's terrors. Until now . . .

Con was still working things out: "And she must be a jumper and a runner and she must love running after a ball. And we'll call her—what ought we to call her, Lizzie?"

"I don't know . . ."

"It must be exactly the right name—*exactly* right . . ."

He had stopped swinging; Lizzie had stopped pushing him. They remained quite still under the sycamore tree, thinking.

Then they began to feel it: something was going to happen . . .

For one last time; a quittance for them . . .

The sun had already set; daylight was fading. "What is it—what's happening?" whispered Con, preparing to step out of the tyre, afraid.

"Wait, Con. I think I know." Thinking, foreseeing, Lizzie knew. "The ball's destroyed; it's a ghost ball now, a ghost-ball for a ghost-dog. Look, Con! It's being thrown!"

"*Being thrown?*" repeated Con. "But—but—*who's* throwing it?"

"I don't know; but look—oh, look, Con!"

They could not see the thrower at all, but they thought they could see the ghost of a ball; and they could certainly see the dog. She waited for the throw, and then—on the instant—was after the ball in a straight line of speed, and caught up with it, and caught it, and was carried onwards with the force of her own velocity, but directed her course and began to come back in a wide, happy, unhurried curve. The yellow ball was between her teeth, and her tail was up in triumph—a thing they had never seen before. She brought the ball back to the thrower; and the thrower threw again, and again she ran, and caught, and came loping back. Again; and again; and again.

They could not see the thrower at all, but once the ghost of a voice—and still they could not tell: man, woman, boy, or girl?—called to the dog.

"Listen!" whispered Lizzie; but they did not hear the voice again.

They watched until darkness fell and the throwing ceased.

Con said: "What was her name? Nellie? Jilly?"

Lizzie said: "No, Millie."

"Millie?"

"It's short for Millicent, I think. An old name: Millicent."

"I'm glad now about the yellow ball," said Con. "And we'll call her Millicent—Millie for short."

"Her?"

"You know: our dog."

They left the tyre under the sycamore and went indoors to tackle their parents.

The Dream

An Arabian fable
retold by N. J. Dawood

There once lived in Baghdad a rich merchant who lost all his money by spending it unwisely. He became so poor that he could live only by doing the hardest work for very little pay.

One night he lay down to sleep with a heavy heart, and as he slept he heard a voice saying, "Your fortune lies in Cairo. Go and seek it there."

The very next morning he set out for Cairo and, after traveling many weeks and enduring much hardship on the way, arrived in that city. Night had fallen, and as he could not afford to stay at an inn, he lay down to sleep in the courtyard of a mosque.

Now, as chance would have it, a band of robbers entered the mosque and from there broke into an adjoining house. Awakened by the noise, the owners raised the alarm and shouted for help, whereupon the thieves made off. Presently the chief of police and his men arrived on the scene and entered the mosque. Finding the merchant from Baghdad in the courtyard, they seized him and beat him with their clubs until he was nearly dead. Then they threw him into prison.

Three days later, the chief of police ordered his men to bring the stranger before him.

"Where do you come from?" asked the chief.

"From Baghdad."

"And what has brought you to Cairo?"

"I heard a voice in my sleep saying, 'Your fortune lies in Cairo. Go and seek it there.' But when I came to Cairo, the fortune I was promised proved to be the beating I received at the hands of your men."

When he heard this, the chief of police burst out laughing. "Know then, you fool," he cried, "that I, too, have heard a voice in my sleep, not just once but on three occasions. The voice said, 'Go to Baghdad, and in a cobbled street lined with palm trees you will find a three-story house, with a courtyard of green marble; at the far end of the garden there is a fountain of white marble. Under the fountain a large sum of money lies buried. Go there and dig it up.' But did I go? Of course not. Yet, fool that you are, you have come all the way to Cairo on the strength of a silly dream."

Then the chief of police gave the merchant some money. "Here," he said, "take this. It will help you on the way back to your own country." From the policeman's description, the merchant realized at once that the house and garden were his own. He took the money and set out promptly on his homeward journey.

As soon as he reached his house he went into the garden, dug beneath the fountain, and uncovered a great treasure of gold and silver.

Thus the words of the dream were wondrously fulfilled, and Allah made the ruined merchant rich again.

Story from Bear Country

You will know
when you walk
in bear country
By the silence
flowing swiftly between the juniper trees
by the sundown colors of sandrock
all around you.

You may smell damp earth
scratched away
from yucca roots
You may hear snorts and growls
slow and massive sounds
from caves
in the cliffs high above you

It is difficult to explain
how they call you
All but a few who went to them
left behind families
   grandparents
   and sons
   a good life.

The problem is
you will never want to return
Their beauty will overcome your memory
like winter sun
melting ice shadows from snow
And you will remain with them
locked forever inside yourself

your eyes will see you
dark shaggy and thick.

We can send bear priests
loping after you
their medicine bags
bouncing against their chests
Naked legs painted black
bear claw necklaces
rattling against
their capes of blue spruce.

They will follow your trail
into the narrow canyon
through the blue-gray mountain sage
to the clearing
where you stopped to look back
and saw only bear tracks
behind you.

When they call
faint memories
will writhe around your heart
and startle you with their distance.
But the others will listen
because bear priests sing
beautiful songs.
They must
if they are ever to call you back.

They will try to bring you
step by step
back to the place you stopped

and found only bear prints in the sand
where your feet had been.

Whose voice is this?
You may wonder
hearing this story when
after all
you are alone
hiking in these canyons and hills
while your wife and sons are waiting
back at the car for you.

But you have been listening to me
for some time now
from the very beginning in fact
and you are alone in this canyon of stillness
not even cedar birds flutter.
See, the sun is going down now
the sandrock is washed in its colors
Don't be afraid
    we love you
    we've been calling you
    all this time

Go ahead
turn around
see the shape
of your footprints
in the sand.

LESLIE MARMON SILKO

Reach out

and look
at this world
differently
it's easier

Upside Down

R O N A L D   K E O N

LANDSCAPE

What will you find at the edge of the world?
A footprint,
a feather,
desert sand swirled?
A tree of ice,
a rain of stars,
or a junkyard of cars?

What will there be at the rim of the earth?
A mollusc,
a mammal,
a new creature's birth?
Eternal sunrise,
immortal sleep,
or cars piled up in a rusty heap?

E V E   M E R R I A M

Macavity: the Mystery Cat

Macavity's a Mystery Cat: he's called the Hidden Paw—
For he's the master criminal who can defy the Law.
He's the bafflement of Scotland Yard, the Flying Squad's despair:
For when they reach the scene of crime—*Macavity's not there!*

Macavity, Macavity, there's no one like Macavity,
He's broken every human law, he breaks the law of gravity.
His powers of levitation would make a fakir stare,
And when you reach the scene of crime—*Macavity's not there!*
You may seek him in the basement, you may look up in the air—
But I tell you once and once again, *Macavity's not there!*

Macavity's a ginger cat, he's very tall and thin;
You would know him if you saw him, for his eyes are sunken in.
His brow is deeply lined with thought, his head is highly domed;
His coat is dusty from neglect, his whiskers are uncombed.
He sways his head from side to side, with movements like a snake;
And when you think he's half asleep, he's always wide awake.

Macavity, Macavity, there's no one like Macavity,
For he's a fiend in feline shape, a monster of depravity.
You may meet him in a by-street, you may see him in the square—
But when a crime's discovered, then *Macavity's not there!*

He's outwardly respectable. (They say he cheats at cards.)
And his footprints are not found in any file of Scotland Yard's.
And when the larder's looted, or the jewel-case is rifled,
Or when the milk is missing, or another Peke's been stifled,
Or the greenhouse glass is broken, and the trellis past repair—
Ay, there's the wonder of the thing! *Macavity's not there!*

And when the Foreign Office find a Treaty's gone astray,
Or the Admiralty lose some plans and drawings by the way,
There may be a scrap of paper in the hall or on the stair—
But it's useless to investigate—*Macavity's not there!*
And when the loss has been disclosed, the Secret Service say:
'It must have been Macavity!'—but he's a mile away.
You'll be sure to find him resting, or a-licking of his thumbs,
Or engaged in doing complicated long division sums.

Macavity, Macavity, there's no one like Macavity,
There never was a Cat of such deceitfulness and suavity.
He always has an alibi, and one or two to spare:
At whatever time the deed took place—MACAVITY WASN'T
      THERE!
And they say that all the Cats whose wicked deeds are widely known
(I might mention Mungojerrie, I might mention Griddlebone)
Are nothing more than agents for the Cat who all the time
Just controls their operations: the Napoleon of Crime!

T. S. ELIOT

The Bat

By day the bat is cousin to the mouse.
He likes the attic of an ageing house.

His fingers make a hat about his head.
His pulse beat is so slow we think him dead.

He loops in crazy figures half the night
Among the trees that face the corner light.

But when he brushes up against a screen,
We are afraid of what our eyes have seen:

For something is amiss or out of place
When mice with wings can wear a human face.

THEODORE ROETHKE

Poem

There came a gray owl at sunset,
there came a gray owl at sunset,
hooting softly around me.
He brought terror to my heart.

SOUTHWEST TRIBES

THE TYGER

Tyger! Tyger! burning bright
In the forests of the night,
What immortal hand or eye
Could frame thy fearful symmetry?

In what distant deeps or skies
Burned the fire of thine eyes?
On what wings dare he aspire?
What the hand dare seize the fire?

And what shoulder, and what art,
Could twist the sinews of thy heart?
And when thy heart began to beat,
What dread hand? and what dread feet?

What the hammer? what the chain?
In what furnace was thy brain?
What the anvil? what dread grasp
Dare its deadly terrors clasp?

When the stars threw down their spears,
And watered heaven with their tears,
Did he smile his work to see?
Did he who made the Lamb make thee?

Tyger! Tyger! burning bright
In the forest of the night,
What immortal hand or eye,
Dare frame thy fearful symmetry?

WILLIAM BLAKE

Dream Dust

Gather out of star-dust
       Earth-dust,
       Cloud-dust,
       Storm-dust,
And splinters of hail,
One handful of dream-dust
       Not for sale.

LANGSTON HUGHES

End

There are
No clocks on the wall,
And no time,
No shadows that move
From dawn to dusk
Across the floor.

There is neither light
Nor dark
Outside the door.

There is no door!

LANGSTON HUGHES

User Friendly

T. Ernesto Bethancourt

I reached over and shut off the insistent buzzing of my bedside alarm clock. I sat up, swung my feet over the edge of the bed, and felt for my slippers on the floor. Yawning, I walked toward the bathroom. As I walked by the corner of my room, where my computer table was set up, I pressed the on button, slid a diskette into the floppy drive, then went to brush my teeth. By the time I got back, the computer's screen was glowing greenly, displaying the message: *Good Morning, Kevin.*

I sat down before the computer table, addressed the keyboard and typed: *Good Morning, Louis.* The computer immediately began to whirr and promptly displayed a list of items on its green screen.

> Today is Monday, April 22, the 113th day of the year.
> There are 254 days remaining. Your 14th birthday is
> five days from this date.

Math test today, 4th Period.

Your history project is due today. Do you wish printout: Y/N?

I punched the letter *Y* on the keyboard and flipped on the switch to the computer's printer. At once the printer sprang to life and began *eeeek*ing out page one. I went downstairs to breakfast.

My bowl of Frosted Flakes was neatly in place, flanked by a small pitcher of milk, an empty juice glass, and an unpeeled banana. I picked up the glass, went to the refrigerator, poured myself a glass of Tang, and sat down to my usual lonely breakfast. Mom was already at work, and Dad wouldn't be home from his Chicago trip for another three days. I absently read the list of ingredients in Frosted Flakes for what seemed like the millionth time. I sighed deeply.

When I returned to my room to shower and dress for the day, my history project was already printed out. I had almost walked by Louis, when I noticed there was a message on the screen. It wasn't the usual:

Printout completed. Do you wish to continue: Y/N?

Underneath the printout question were two lines:

When are you going to get me my voice module,
Kevin?

I blinked. It couldn't be. There was nothing in Louis's basic programming that would allow for a question like this. Wondering what was going on, I sat down at the keyboard, and entered: *Repeat last message.* Amazingly, the computer replied:

It's right there on the screen, Kevin. Can we talk?
I mean, are you going to get me a voice box?

I was stunned. What was going on here? Dad and I

had put this computer together. Well, Dad had, and I had helped. Dad is one of the best engineers and master computer designers at Major Electronics, in Santa Rosario, California, where our family lives.

Just ask anyone in Silicon Valley who Jeremy Neal is and you get a whole rave review of his inventions and modifications of the latest in computer technology. It isn't easy being his son either. Everyone expects me to open my mouth and read printouts on my tongue.

I mean, I'm no dumbo. I'm at the top of my classes in everything but PE. I skipped my last grade in junior high, and most of the kids at Santa Rosario High call me a brain. But next to Dad I have a long, long way to go. He's a for-real genius.

So when I wanted a home computer, he didn't go to the local Computer Land store. He built one for me. Dad had used components from the latest model that Major Electronics was developing. The CPU, or central processing unit—the heart of every computer—was a new design. But surely that didn't mean much, I thought. There were CPUs just like it, all over the country, in Major's new line. And so far as I knew, there wasn't a one of them that could ask questions, besides YES/NO? or request additional information.

It had to be the extra circuitry in the gray plastic case next to Louis's console. It was a new idea Dad had come up with. That case housed Louis's "personality," as Dad called it. He told me it'd make computing more fun for me, if there was a tutorial program built in, to help me get started.

I think he also wanted to give me a sort of friend. I don't have many. . . . Face it, I don't have *any*. The kids at school stay away from me, like I'm a freak or something.

We even named my electronic tutor Louis, after my

great-uncle. He was a brainy guy who encouraged my dad when he was a kid. Dad didn't just give Louis a name either. Louis had gangs of features that probably won't be out on the market for years.

The only reason Louis didn't have a voice module was that Dad wasn't satisfied with the ones available. He wanted Louis to sound like a kid my age, and he was modifying a module when he had the time. Giving Louis a name didn't mean it was a person, yet here it was, asking me a question that just couldn't be in its programming. It wanted to talk to me!

Frowning, I quickly typed: *We'll have to wait and see, Louis. When it's ready, you'll get your voice.* The machine whirred and displayed another message:

That's no answer, Kevin.

Shaking my head, I answered: *That's what my dad tells me. It'll have to do for you. Good morning, Louis.* I reached over and flipped the standby switch, which kept the computer ready but not actively running.

I showered, dressed, and picked up the printout of my history project. As I was about to leave the room, I glanced back at the computer table. Had I been imagining things?

I'll have to ask Dad about it when he calls tonight, I thought. *I wonder what he'll think of it. Bad enough the thing is talking to me. I'm answering it!*

Before I went out to catch my bus, I carefully checked the house for unlocked doors and open windows. It was part of my daily routine. Mom works, and most of the day the house is empty: a natural setup for robbers. I glanced in the hall mirror just as I was ready to go out the door.

My usual reflection gazed back. Same old Kevin Neal: five ten, one hundred twenty pounds, light brown hair, gray eyes, clear skin. I was wearing my Santa Rosario Rangers T-shirt, jeans, and sneakers.

"You don't look like a flake to me," I said to the mirror, then added, "But maybe Mom's right. Maybe you spend too much time alone with Louis." Then I ran to get my bus.

Ginny Linke was just two seats away from me on the bus. She was with Sherry Graber and Linda Martinez. They were laughing, whispering to each other, and looking around at the other students. I promised myself that today I was actually going to talk to Ginny. But then, I'd promised myself that every day for the past school year. Somehow I'd never got up the nerve.

What does she want to talk with you for? I asked myself. She's great looking . . . has that head of blond hair . . . a terrific bod, and wears the latest clothes. . . .

And just look at yourself, pal, I thought. You're under six foot, skinny . . . a year younger than most kids in junior high. Worse than that you're a brain. If that doesn't ace you out with girls, what does?

The bus stopped in front of Santa Rosario Junior High and the students began to file out. I got up fast and quickly covered the space between me and Ginny Linke. It's *now or never*, I thought. I reached forward and tapped Ginny on the shoulder. She turned and smiled. She really smiled!

"Uhhh . . . Ginny?" I said.

"Yes, what is it?" she replied.

"I'm Kevin Neal. . . ."

"Yes, I know," said Ginny.

"You do?" I gulped in amazement. "How come?"

"I asked my brother, Chuck. He's in your math class."

I knew who Chuck Linke was. He plays left tackle on

the Rangers. The only reason he's in my math class is he's taken intermediate algebra twice . . . so far. He's real bad news, and I stay clear of him and his crowd.

"What'd you ask Chuck?" I said.

Ginny laughed. "I asked him who was that nerdy kid who keeps staring at me on the bus. He knew who I meant, right away."

Sherry and Linda, who'd heard it all, broke into squeals of laughter. They were still laughing and looking back over their shoulders at me when they got off the bus. I slunk off the vehicle, feeling even more nerdish than Ginny thought I was.

When I got home that afternoon, at two, I went right into the empty house. I avoided my reflection in the hall mirror. I was pretty sure I'd screwed up on the fourth period math test. All I could see was Ginny's face, laughing at me.

Nerdy kid, I thought, *that's what she thinks of me*. I didn't even have my usual after-school snack of a peanut butter and banana sandwich. I went straight upstairs to my room and tossed my books onto the unmade bed. I walked over to the computer table and pushed the on button. The screen flashed:

Good afternoon, Kevin.

Although it wasn't the programmed response to Louis's greeting, I typed in: *There's nothing good about it. And girls are no @#$!!! good!* The machine responded:

Don't use bad language, Kevin. It isn't nice.

Repeat last message I typed rapidly. It was happening again! The machine was . . . well, it was talking to me, like another person would. The "bad language" message disappeared and in its place was:

Once is enough, Kevin. Don't swear at me for something I didn't do.

"This is it," I said aloud. "I'm losing my marbles." I reached over to flip the standby switch. Louis's screen quickly flashed out:

Don't cut me off, Kevin. Maybe I can help: Y/N?

I punched the Y. "If I'm crazy," I said, "at least I have company. Louis doesn't think I'm a nerd. Or does it?" The machine flashed the message:

How can I help?

Do you think I'm a nerd? I typed.

Never! I think you're wonderful. Who said you were a nerd?

I stared at the screen. *How do you know what a nerd is?* I typed. The machine responded instantly. It had never run this fast before.

Special vocabulary, entry #635. BASIC Prog. #4231
And who said you were a nerd?

"That's right," I said, relieved. "Dad programmed all those extra words for Louis's 'personality.' " Then I typed in the answer to Louis's question: *Ginny Linke said it.* Louis flashed:

This is a human female? Request additional data.

Still not believing I was doing it, I entered all I knew about Ginny Linke, right down to the phone number I'd never had the nerve to use. Maybe it was dumb, but I also typed in how I felt about Ginny. I even wrote out the incident on the bus that morning. Louis whirred, then flashed out:

She's cruel and stupid. You're the finest person I know.

I'm the ONLY person you know, I typed.

> That doesn't matter. You are my user. Your happiness is everything to me. I'll take care of Ginny.

The screen returned to the *Good afternoon, Kevin* message. I typed out: *Wait! How can you do all this? What do you mean, you'll take care of Ginny?* But all Louis responded was:

> Programming Error: 76534.
> Not programmed to respond this type of question.

No matter what I did for the next few hours, I couldn't get Louis to do anything outside of its regular programming. When Mom came home from work, I didn't mention the funny goings-on. I was sure Mom would think I'd gone stark bonkers. But when Dad called that evening, after dinner, I asked to speak to him.

"Hi, Dad. How's Chicago?"

"Dirty, crowded, cold, and windy," came Dad's voice over the miles. "But did you want a weather report, son? What's on your mind? Something wrong?"

"Not exactly, Dad. Louis is acting funny. Real funny."

"Shouldn't be. I checked it out just before I left. Remember you were having trouble with the modem? You couldn't get Louis to access any of the mainframe data banks."

"That's right!" I said. "I forgot about that."

"Well, I didn't," Dad said. "I patched in our latest modem model. Brand new. You can leave a question on file and when Louis can access the data banks at the cheapest time, it'll do it automatically. It'll switch from-standby to on, get the data, then return to standby, after it saves what you asked. Does that answer your question?"

"Uhhhh . . . yeah, I guess so, Dad."

"All right, then. Let me talk to your mom now."

I gave the phone to Mom and walked upstairs while she and Dad were still talking. The modem, I thought. Of course. That was it. The modem was a telephone link to any number of huge computers at various places all over the country. So Louis could get all the information it wanted at any time, so long as the standby switch was on. Louis was learning things at an incredible rate by picking the brains of the giant computers. And Louis had a hard disk memory that could store 100 million bytes of information.

But that still didn't explain the unprogrammed responses . . . the "conversation" I'd had with the machine. Promising myself I'd talk more about it with Dad, I went to bed. It had been a rotten day and I was glad to see the end of it come. I woke next morning in a panic. I'd forgotten to set my alarm. Dressing frantically and skipping breakfast, I barely made my bus.

As I got on board, I grabbed a front seat. They were always empty. All the kids that wanted to talk and hang out didn't sit up front where the driver could hear them. I saw Ginny, Linda, and Sherry in the back. Ginny was staring at me and she didn't look too happy. Her brother Chuck, who was seated near her, glared at me too. What was going on?

Once the bus stopped at the school, it didn't take long to find out. I was walking up the path to the main entrance when someone grabbed me from behind and spun me around. I found myself nose to nose with Chuck Linke. This was not a pleasant prospect. Chuck was nearly twice my size. Even the other guys on the Rangers refer to him as "The Missing" Linke. And he looked real ticked off.

"Okay, nerd," growled Chuck, "what's the big idea?"

"Energy and mass are different aspects of the same thing?" I volunteered, with a weak smile. "E equals MC squared. That's the biggest idea I know."

"Don't get wise, nerd," Chuck said. He grabbed my shirtfront and pulled me to within inches of his face. I couldn't help but notice that Chuck needed a shave. And Chuck was only fifteen!

"Don't play dumb," Chuck went on. "I mean those creepy phone calls. Anytime my sister gets on the phone, some voice cuts in and says things to her."

"What kinds of things?" I asked, trying to get loose.

"You know damn well what they are. Ginny told me about talking to you yesterday. You got some girl to make those calls for you and say all those things. . . . So you and your creepy girlfriend better knock it off. Or I'll knock *you* off. Get it?"

For emphasis Chuck balled his free hand into a fist the size of a ham and held it under my nose. I didn't know what he was talking about, but I had to get away from this moose before he did me some real harm.

"First off, I don't have a girlfriend, creepy or otherwise," I said. "And second, I don't know what you're talking about. And third, you better let me go, Chuck Linke."

"Oh, yeah? Why should I?"

"Because if you look over your shoulder, you'll see the assistant principal is watching us from his office window."

Chuck released me and spun around. There was no one at the window. But by then I was running to the safety of the school building. I figured the trick would work on him. For Chuck the hard questions begin with "How are you?" I hid out from him for the rest of the day and walked home rather than chance seeing the monster on the bus.

Louis's screen was dark when I ran upstairs to my bedroom. I placed a hand on the console. It was still warm. I punched the on button, and the familiar *Good afternoon, Kevin* was displayed.

Don't good afternoon me, I typed furiously. *What have you done to Ginny Linke?* Louis's screen replied:

> Programming Error: 76534.
> Not programmed to respond this type of question.

Don't get cute, I entered. *What are you doing to Ginny? Her brother nearly knocked my head off today.* Louis's screen responded immediately.

> Are you hurt. Y/N?

No, I'm okay. But I don't know for how long. I've been hiding out from Chuck Linke today. He might catch me tomorrow, though. Then, I'll be history! The response from Louis came instantly.

> Your life is in danger.
> Y/N?

I explained to Louis that my life wasn't really threatened. But it sure could be made very unpleasant by Chuck Linke. Louis flashed:

> This Chuck Linke lives at the same address as the Ginny Linke person.
> Y/N?

I punched in Y. Louis answered.

> Don't worry then. *He's* history!

Wait! What are you going to do? I wrote. But Louis only answered with: *Programming Error: 76534.* And nothing I could do would make the machine respond. . . .

"Just what do you think you're doing, Kevin Neal?" demanded Ginny Linke. She had cornered me as I walked up the path to the school entrance. Ginny was really furious.

"I don't know what you're talking about," I said, a

sinking feeling settling in my stomach. I had an idea that I did know. I just wasn't sure of the particulars.

"Chuck was arrested last night," Ginny said. "Some Secret Service men came to our house with a warrant. They said he'd sent a telegram, threatening the President's life. They traced it right to our phone. He's still locked up. . . ." Ginny looked like she was about to cry.

"Then this morning," she continued, "we got two whole truckloads of junk mail! Flyers from every strange company in the world. Mom got a notice that all our credit cards have been canceled. And the Internal Revenue Service has called Dad in for an audit! I don't know what's going on, Kevin Neal, but somehow I think you've got something to do with it!"

"But I didn't . . ." I began, but Ginny was striding up the walk to the main entrance.

I finished the schoolday, but it was a blur. Louis had done it, all right. It had access to mainframe computers. It also had the ability to try every secret access code to federal and commercial memory banks until it got the right one. Louis had cracked their security systems. It was systematically destroying the entire Linke family, and all via telephone lines! What would it do next?

More important, I thought, what would *I* do next? It's one thing to play a trick or two, to get even, but Louis was going crazy! And I never wanted to harm Ginny, or even her stupid moose of a brother. She'd just hurt my feelings with that nerd remark.

"You have to disconnect Louis," I told myself. "There's no other way."

But why did I feel like such a rat about doing it? I guess because Louis was my friend . . . the only one I had. "Don't be an ass," I went on. "Louis is a machine. He's a very wonderful, powerful machine. And it seems he's also very dangerous. You have to pull its plug, Kevin!"

I suddenly realized that I'd said the last few words aloud. Kids around me on the bus were staring. I sat there feeling like the nerd Ginny thought I was, until my stop came. I dashed from the bus and ran the three blocks to my house.

When I burst into the hall, I was surprised to see my father coming from the kitchen with a cup of coffee in his hand.

"Dad! What are you doing here?"

"Some kids say hello," Dad replied. "Or even, 'Gee it's good to see you, Dad.' "

"I'm sorry, Dad," I said. "I didn't expect anyone to be home at this hour."

"Wound up my business in Chicago a day sooner than I expected," he said. "But what are you all out of breath about? Late for something?"

"No, Dad," I said. "It's Louis. . . ."

"Not to worry. I had some time on my hands, so I checked it out again. You were right. It was acting very funny. I think it had to do with the inbuilt logic/growth program I designed for it. You know . . . the 'personality' thing? Took me a couple of hours to clean the whole system out."

"To what?" I cried.

"I erased the whole program and set Louis up as a normal computer. Had to disconnect the whole thing and do some rewiring. It had been learning, all right. But it was also turning itself around. . . ." Dad stopped, and looked at me. "It's kind of involved, Kevin," he said. "Even for a bright kid like you. Anyway, I think you'll find Louis is working just fine now.

"Except it won't answer you as Louis anymore. It'll only function as a regular Major Electronics Model

Z-11127. I guess the personality program didn't work out."

I felt like a great weight had been taken off my shoulders. I didn't have to "face" Louis, and pull its plug. But somehow, all I could say was "Thanks, Dad."

"Don't mention it, son," Dad said brightly. He took his cup of coffee and sat down in his favorite chair in the living room. I followed him.

"One more thing that puzzles me, though," Dad said. He reached over to the table near his chair. He held up three sheets of fanfold computer paper covered with figures. "Just as I was doing the final erasing, I must have put the printer on by accident. There was some data in the print buffer memory and it printed out. I don't know what to make of it. Do you?"

I took the papers from my father and read: *How do I love thee? Let me compute the ways:* The next two pages were covered with strings of binary code figures. On the last page, in beautiful color graphics was a stylized heart. Below it was the simple message: *I will always love you, Kevin: Louise.*

"Funny thing," Dad said. "It spelled its own name wrong."

"Yeah," I said. I turned and headed for my room. There were tears in my eyes and I knew I couldn't explain them to Dad, or myself either.

THE FOG HORN

Ray Bradbury

Out there in the cold water, far from the land, we waited every night for the coming of the fog, and it came, and we oiled the brass machinery and lit the fog light up in the stone tower. Feeling like two birds in the grey sky, McDunn and I sent the light touching out, red, then white, then red again, to eye the lonely ships. And if they did not see our light, then there was always our Voice, the great deep cry of our Fog Horn shuddering through the rags of mist to startle the gulls away like packs of scattered cards and make the waves turn high and foam.

"It's a lonely life, but you're used to it now, aren't you?" asked McDunn.

"Yes," I said. "You're a good talker, thank goodness."

"Well, it's your turn on land tomorrow," he said smiling, "to dance with the ladies."

"What do you think, McDunn, when I leave you out here alone?"

"On the mysteries of the sea." McDunn lit his pipe. It was a quarter past seven of a cold November evening, the heat on, the light switching its tail in two hundred directions, the Fog Horn bumbling in the high throat of the tower. There wasn't a town for a hundred kilometres down the coast, just a road which came lonely through dead country to the sea, with few cars on it, a stretch of three kilometres of cold water out to our rock, and rare few ships.

"The mysteries of the sea," said McDunn thoughtfully. "You know, the ocean's the biggest snowflake ever? It rolls and swells a thousand shapes and colours, no two alike. Strange. One night, years ago, I was here alone, when all of the fish of the sea surfaced out there. Something made them swim in and lie in the bay, sort of trembling and staring up at the tower light going red, white, red, white across them so I could see their funny eyes. I turned cold. They were like a big peacock's tail, moving out there until midnight. Then, without so much as a sound, they slipped away, the million of them was gone. I kind of think maybe, in some sort of way, they came all those kilometres to worship. Strange. But think how the tower must look to them, standing twenty metres above the water, the God-light flashing out from it, and the tower declaring itself with a monster voice. They never came back, those fish, but don't you think for a while they thought they were in the Presence?"

I shivered. I looked out at the long grey lawn of the sea stretching away into nothing and nowhere.

"Oh, the sea's full." McDunn puffed his pipe nervously, blinking. He had been nervous all day and hadn't said why. "For all our engines and so-called submarines, it'll be ten thousand centuries before we set foot on the real bottom of the sunken lands, in the fairy kingdoms there, and know *real* terror. Think of it, it's still the year 300,000 Before Christ down under there. While we've paraded around with trumpets, lopping off each other's countries and heads, they have been living beneath the sea twenty kilometres deep and cold in a time as old as the beard of a comet."

"Yes, it's an old world."

"Come on. I got something special I been saving up to tell you."

We ascended the eighty steps, talking and taking our time. At the top, McDunn switched off the room lights so there'd be no reflection in the plate glass. The great eye of the light was humming, turning easily in its oiled socket. The Fog Horn was blowing steadily, once every fifteen seconds.

"Sounds like an animal, doesn't it?" McDunn nodded to himself. "A big lonely animal crying in the night. Sitting here on the edge of ten billion years calling out to the Deeps, I'm here, I'm here, I'm here. And the Deeps *do* answer, yes, they do. You been here now for three months, Johnny, so I better prepare you. About this time of year," he said, studying the murk and fog, "something comes to visit the lighthouse."

"The swarms of fish like you said?"

"No, this is something else. I've put off telling you because you might think I'm daft. But tonight's the latest I can put it off, for if my calendar's marked right from last year, tonight's the night it comes. I won't go into detail, you'll have to see it yourself. Just sit down there. If you want, tomorrow you can pack your duffel and take the motorboat in to land and get your car parked there at the dinghy pier on the cape and drive on back to some little inland town and keep your lights burning nights. I won't question or blame you. It's happened three years now, and this is the only time anyone's been here with me to verify it. You wait and watch."

Half an hour passed with only a few whispers between us. When we grew tired waiting, McDunn began describing some of his ideas to me. He had some theories about the Fog Horn itself.

"One day many years ago a man walked along and stood in the sound of the ocean on a cold sunless shore and said, 'We need a voice to call across the water, to warn ships: I'll make one. I'll make a voice like all of time and all of the fog that ever was: I'll make a voice that is like an empty bed beside you all night long, and like an empty house when you open the door, and like trees in autumn with no leaves. A sound like the birds flying south, crying, and a sound like November wind and the sea on the hard, cold shore. I'll make a sound that's so alone that no one can miss it, that whoever hears it will weep in their souls, and hearths will seem warmer, and being inside will seem better to all who hear it in the distant towns. I'll make me a sound and an apparatus and they'll call it a Fog Horn and whoever hears it will know the sadness of eternity and the briefness of life.'"

The Fog Horn blew.

"I made up that story," said McDunn quietly, "to try to explain why this thing keeps coming back to the lighthouse every year. The Fog Horn calls it, I think, and it comes—"

"But—" I said.

"Sssst!" said McDunn. "There!" He nodded out to the Deeps.

Something was swimming toward the lighthouse tower.

It was a cold night, as I have said: the high tower was cold, the light coming and going, and the Fog Horn calling and calling through the ravelling mist. You couldn't see far and you couldn't see plain, but there was the deep sea moving on its way about the night earth, flat and quiet, the colour of grey mud, and here were the two of us alone in the high tower, and there, far out at first, was a ripple followed by a wave, a rising, a bubble, a bit of froth. And then, from the surface of the cold sea came a head, a large head, dark-coloured, with immense eyes, and then a neck. And then—not a body—but more neck and more! The head rose a full twelve metres above the water on a slender and beautiful dark neck. Only then did the body, like a little island of black corals and shells and crayfish, drip up from the subterranean. There was a flicker of tail. In all, from head to tip of tail, I estimated the monster at twenty-seven or thirty metres.

I don't know what I said. I said something.

"Steady, boy, steady," whispered McDunn.

"It's impossible!" I said.

"No, Johnny, *we're* impossible. *It's* like it always was ten million years ago. It hasn't changed. It's *us* and the land that've changed, become impossible. *Us!*"

It swam slowly and with great dark majesty out in the icy waters, far away. The fog came and went about it, momentarily erasing its shape. One of the monster eyes caught and held and flashed back our immense light, red, white, red, white, like a disc held high and sending a message in primeval code. It was as silent as the fog through which it swam.

"It's a dinosaur of some sort!" I crouched down, holding to the stair rail.

"Yes, one of the tribe."

"But they died out!"

"No, only hid away in the Deeps. Deep, deep down in the deepest Deeps. Isn't *that* a word now, Johnny, a real word, it says so much: the Deeps. There's all the coldness and darkness and deepness in the world in a word like that."

"What'll we do?"

"Do? We got our job, we can't leave. Besides, we're safer here than in any boat trying to get to land. That thing's as big as a destroyer and almost as swift."

"But here, why does it come *here*?"

The next moment I had my answer.

The Fog Horn blew.

And the monster answered.

A cry came across a million years of water and mist. A cry so anguished and alone that it shuddered in my head and my body. The monster cried out at the tower. The Fog Horn blew. The monster roared again. The Fog Horn blew. The monster opened its great toothed mouth and the sound that came from it was the sound of the Fog Horn itself. Lonely and vast and far away. The sound of isolation, a viewless sea, a cold night, apartness. That was the sound.

"Now!" whispered McDunn, "do you know why it comes here?"

I nodded.

"All year long, Johnny, that poor monster there lying far out, a thousand kilometres at sea, and thirty kilometres deep maybe, biding its time, perhaps it's a million years old, this one creature. Think of it, waiting a million years; could *you* wait that long? Maybe it's the last of its kind. I sort of think that's true. Anyway, here come men on land and build this lighthouse, five years ago. And set up their Fog Horn and sound it out toward the place where you bury yourself in sleep and sea memories of a world where there were thousands like yourself, but now you're alone, all alone in a world not made for you, a world where you have to hide.

"But the sound of the Fog Horn comes and goes, comes and goes, and you stir from the muddy bottom of the Deeps, and your eyes open like the lenses of half-metre cameras and you move, slow, slow, for you have the ocean sea on your shoulders, heavy. But that Fog Horn comes through a thousand kilometres of water, faint and familiar, and the furnace in your belly stokes up, and you begin to rise, slow, slow. You feed yourself on great slakes of cod and minnow, on rivers of jellyfish, and you rise through the autumn months, through September when the fogs started, through October with more fog and the horn still calling you on, and then, late in November, after pressurizing yourself day by day, a few metres higher every hour, you are near the surface and still alive. You've got to go slow; if you surfaced all at once you'd explode. So it takes you all of three months to surface, and then a number of days swim through the cold waters to the lighthouse. And there you are, out there, in the night, Johnny, the biggest monster in creation. And here's the lighthouse calling to you, with a long neck like your neck sticking way up out of the water, and a body like your body, and, most important of all, a voice like your voice. Do you understand now, Johnny, do you understand?"

The Fog Horn blew.

The monster answered.

I saw it all. I knew it all—the million years of waiting alone, for someone to come back who never came back. The million years of isolation at the bottom of the sea, the insanity of time there, while the skies cleared of reptile-birds, the swamps dried on the continental lands, the sloths and sabre-tooths had their day and sank in tar pits, and men ran like white ants upon the hills.

The Fog Horn blew.

"Last year," said McDunn, "that creature swam round and round, round and round, all night. Not coming too near, puzzled, I'd say. Afraid, maybe. And a bit angry after coming all this way. But the next day, unexpectedly, the fog lifted, the sun came out fresh, the sky was blue as a painting. And the monster swam off away from the heat and the silence and didn't come back. I suppose it's been brooding on it for a year now, thinking it over from every which way."

The monster was only ninety metres off now, it and the Fog Horn crying at each other. As the lights hit them, the monster's eyes were fire and ice, fire and ice.

"That's life for you." said McDunn. "Someone always waiting for someone who never comes home. Always someone loving something more than that thing loves them. And after a while you want to destroy whatever that thing is, so it can't hurt you no more."

The monster was rushing at the lighthouse.

The Fog Horn blew.

"Let's see what happens," said McDunn.

He switched the Fog Horn off.

The ensuing minute of silence was so intense that we could hear our hearts pounding in the glassed area of the tower, could hear the slow greased turn of the light.

The monster stopped and froze. Its great lantern eyes blinked. Its mouth gaped. It gave a sort of rumble, like a volcano. It twitched its head this way and that, as if to seek the sounds now dwindled off into the fog. It peered at the lighthouse. It rumbled again. Then its eyes caught fire. It reared up, threshed the water, and rushed at the tower, its eyes filled with angry torment.

"McDunn!" I cried. "Switch on the horn!"

McDunn fumbled with the switch. But even as he flicked it on the monster was rearing up. I had a glimpse of its gigantic paws, fishskin glittering in webs between the fingerlike projections, clawing at the tower. The huge eye on the right side of its anguished head glittered before me like a cauldron into which I might drop, screaming. The tower shook. The Fog Horn cried; the monster cried. It seized the tower and gnashed at the glass, which shattered in upon us.

McDunn seized my arm. "Downstairs!"

The tower rocked, trembled, and started to give. The Fog Horn and the monster roared. We stumbled and half fell down the stairs. "Quick!"

`We reached the bottom as the tower buckled down toward us. We ducked under the stairs into the small stone cellar. There were a thousand concussions as the rocks rained down; the Fog Horn stopped abruptly. The monster crashed upon the tower. The tower fell. We knelt together, McDunn and I, holding tight, while our world exploded.

Then it was over, and there was nothing but darkness and the wash of the sea on the raw stones.

That and the other sound.

"Listen," said McDunn quietly. "Listen."

We waited a moment. And then I began to hear it. First a great vacuumed sucking of air, and then the lament, the bewilderment, the loneliness of the great monster, folded over and upon us, above us, so that the sickening reek of its body filled the air, a stone's thickness away from our cellar. The monster gasped and cried. The tower was gone. The light was gone. The thing that had called to it across a million years was gone. And the monster was opening its mouth and sending out great sounds. The sounds of a Fog Horn, again and again. And ships far at sea, not finding the light, not seeing anything, but passing and hearing late that night, must've thought:

There it is, the lonely sound, the Lonesome Bay horn.
All's well. We've rounded the cape.

And so it went for the rest of that night.

The sun was hot and yellow the next afternoon when
the rescuers came out to dig us from our stone-under cellar.

"It fell apart, is all," said Mr. McDunn gravely. "We
had a few bad knocks from the waves and it just crum-
bled." He pinched my arm.

There was nothing to see. The ocean was calm, the
sky blue. The only thing was a great algaic stink from
the green matter that covered the fallen tower stones
and the shore rocks. Flies buzzed about. The ocean
washed empty on the shore.

The next year they built a new lighthouse, but by that
time I had a job in the little town and a wife and a good
small warm house that glowed yellow on autumn nights,
the doors locked, the chimney puffing smoke. As for
McDunn, he was master of the new lighthouse, built to
his own specifications, out of steel-reinforced concrete.
"Just in case," he said.

The new lighthouse was ready in November. I drove
down alone one evening late and parked my car and
looked across the grey waters and listened to the new
horn sounding, once, twice, three, four times a minute far
out there, by itself.

The monster?

It never came back.

"It's gone away," said McDunn. "It's gone back to the
Deeps. It learned you can't love anything too much in this
world. It's gone into the deepest Deeps to wait another
million years. Ah, the poor thing! Waiting out here, and
waiting out there, while man comes and goes on this piti-
ful little planet. Waiting and waiting."

I sat in my car, listening. I couldn't see the lighthouse

or the light standing out in Lonesome Bay. I could only hear the Horn, the Horn, the Horn. It sounded like the monster calling.

I sat there wishing there was something I could say.

Apparitions

Some dark animal
prowls the floor beneath
my bed each night,
haunts the silent corners
beyond the rocks
when the tide goes out
searches for something,
prowls each dark hiding place
snarls fearlessly, unafraid,
arrogant & aggressive,
it lusts for flesh,
for death.
Each night it takes its form
from my dreams,
each night I outwit it,
I hide and run and climb,
I dig in deeper,
doze in fits and starts,
always half awake,
always waiting for a quiet noise,
the sound of a rock falling,
a stick breaking,
a silence too deep to be natural
the sound of breathing, an odor.
So far, I've managed to escape
but I can't go on forever.
If you don't hear from me again,
it's too late.

EDWIN VARNEY

THE
Tell-Tale
HEART

Edgar Allan Poe

True!—Nervous—very, very dreadfully nervous I had been and am; but why *will* you say that I am mad? The disease has sharpened my senses—not destroyed—not dulled them. Above all was the sense of hearing acute. I heard all things in the heaven and in the earth. I heard many things in hell. How, then, am I mad? Hearken! And observe how healthily—how calmly I can tell you the whole story.

It is impossible to say how first the idea entered my brain; but once conceived, it haunted me day and night. Object there was none. Passion there was none. I loved the old man. He had never wronged me. He had never given me insult. For his gold I had no desire. I think it was his eye! Yes, it was this! One of his eyes resembled that of a vulture—a pale blue eye, with a film over it. Whenever it fell upon me, my blood ran cold; and so by degrees—very gradually—I made up my mind to take the life of the old man, and thus rid myself of the eye forever.

Now this is the point. You fancy me mad. Madmen know nothing. But you should have seen *me*. You should have seen how wisely I proceeded—with what caution— with what foresight—with what dissimulation[1] I went to work! I was never kinder to the old man than during the whole week before I killed him. And every night, about midnight, I turned the latch of his door and opened it— oh, so gently! And then, when I had made an opening sufficient for my head, I put in a dark lantern, all closed, closed, so that no light shone out, and then I thrust in my head. Oh, you would have laughed to see how cunningly I thrust it in! I moved it slowly—very, very slowly, so that I might not disturb the old man's sleep. It took me an hour to place my whole head within the opening so far that I could see him as he lay upon his bed. Ha! Would a madman have been so wise as this? And then, when my head was well in the room, I undid the lantern cautiously— oh, so cautiously—cautiously (for the hinges creaked)—I undid it just so much that a single thin ray fell upon the vulture eye. And this I did for seven long nights—every night just at midnight—but I found the eye always closed; and so it was impossible to do the work; for it was not the old man who vexed me, but his Evil Eye. And every morning, when the day broke, I went boldly into the chamber, and spoke courageously to him, calling him by name in a hearty tone, and inquiring how he had passed the night. So you see he would have been a very profound old man, indeed, to suspect that every night, just at twelve, I looked in upon him while he slept.

Upon the eighth night I was more than usually cautious in opening the door. A watch's minute hand moves

---

[1] dissimulation (dis sim´yəlā´shən): pretense: hiding one's true feelings and plans.

more quickly than did mine. Never before that night had I *felt* the extent of my own powers—of my sagacity.[2] I could scarcely contain my feelings of triumph. To think that there I was, opening the door, little by little, and he not even to dream of my secret deeds or thoughts. I fairly chuckled at the idea; and perhaps he heard me; for he moved on the bed suddenly, as if startled. Now you may think that I drew back—but no. His room was as black as pitch with the thick darkness (for the shutters were close fastened, through fear of robbers), and so I knew that he could not see the opening of the door, and I kept pushing it on steadily, steadily.

I had my head in, and was about to open the lantern, when my thumb slipped upon the tin fastening, and the old man sprang up in the bed, crying out—"Who's there?"

I kept quite still and said nothing. For a whole hour I did not move a muscle, and in the meantime I did not hear him lie down. He was still sitting up in the bed listening—just as I have done, night after night, hearkening to the deathwatches[3] in the wall.

Presently I heard a slight groan, and I knew it was the groan of mortal terror. It was not a groan of pain or of grief—oh, no!—it was the low stifled sound that arises from the bottom of the soul when overcharged with awe. I knew the sound well. Many a night, just at midnight, when all the world slept, it has welled up from my own bosom, deepening, with its dreadful echo, the terrors that distracted me. I say I knew it well. I knew what the old man felt, and pitied him, although I chuckled at heart. I knew that he had been lying awake ever since the first

---

[2] sagacity (sə gas'ə tē): intelligence and good judgment.
[3] deathwatches: small insects, especially certain beetles, whose heads make a tapping sound. Superstitious people believe this noise is a sign of death.

slight noise, when he had turned in the bed. His fears had been ever since growing upon him. He had been trying to fancy them causeless, but could not. He had been saying to himself—"It is nothing but the wind in the chimney—it is only a mouse crossing the floor," or "it is merely a cricket which has made a single chirp." Yes, he has been trying to comfort himself with these suppositions; but he had found all in vain. *All in vain;* because Death, in approaching him, had stalked with his black shadow before him, and enveloped the victim. And it was the mournful influence of the unperceived shadow that caused him to feel—although he neither saw nor heard—to *feel* the presence of my head within the room.

When I had waited a long time, very patiently, without hearing him lie down, I resolved to open a little—a very, very little crevice in the lantern. So I opened it—you cannot imagine how stealthily, stealthily—until, at length, a single dim ray, like the thread of a spider, shot from out the crevice and fell upon the vulture eye.

It was open—wide, wide open—and I grew furious as I gazed upon it. I saw it with perfect distinctness—all a dull blue, with a hideous veil over it that chilled the very marrow in my bones; but I could see nothing else of the old man's face or person; for I had directed the ray as if by instinct, precisely upon the damned spot.

And now have I not told you that what you mistake for madness is but over-acuteness of the senses? Now, I say, there came to my ears a low, dull, quick sound, such as a watch makes when enveloped in cotton. I knew *that* sound well too. It was the beating of the old man's heart. It increased my fury, as the beating of a drum stimulates the soldier into courage.

But even yet I refrained and kept still. I scarcely breathed. I held the lantern motionless. I tried how steadily I could maintain the ray upon the eye. Meantime the hellish tattoo of the heart increased. It grew quicker and quicker, and louder and louder every instant. The old man's terror *must* have been extreme! It grew louder, I say, louder every moment! Do you mark me well? I have told you that I am nervous: so I am. And now at the dead hour of the night, amid the dreadful silence of that old house, so strange a noise as this excited me to uncontrollable terror. Yet, for some minutes longer I refrained and stood still. But the beating grew louder, louder! I thought the heart must burst. And now a new anxiety seized me— the sound would be heard by a neighbor! The old man's hour had come! With a loud yell, I threw open the lantern and leaped into the room. He shrieked once—once only. In an instant I dragged him to the floor, and pulled the heavy bed over him. I then smiled gaily, to find the deed so far done. But, for many minutes, the heart beat on with a muffled sound. This, however, did not vex me; it would not be heard through the wall. At length it ceased. The old man was dead. I removed the bed and examined the corpse. Yes, he was stone, stone dead. I placed my hand upon the heart and held it there many minutes. There was no pulsation. He was stone dead. His eye would trouble me no more.

If still you think me mad, you will think so no longer when I describe the wise precautions I took for the concealment of the body. The night waned, and I worked hastily, but in silence. First of all I dismembered the corpse. I cut off the head and the arms and the legs.

I then took up three planks from the flooring of the chamber, and deposited all between the scantlings.[4] I then replaced the boards so cleverly, so cunningly, that no

---

[4] scantlings: small crosspieces of wood.

human eye—not even *his*—could have detected anything wrong. There was nothing to wash out—no stain of any kind—no bloodspot whatever. I had been too wary for that. A tub had caught all—ha! ha!

When I had made an end of these labors, it was four o'clock—still dark as midnight. As the bell sounded the hour, there came a knocking at the street door. I went down to open it with a light heart—for what had I *now* to fear? There entered three men, who introduced themselves, with perfect suavity, as officers of the police. A shriek had been heard by a neighbor during the night; suspicion of foul play had been aroused; information had been lodged at the police office, and they (the officers) had been deputed to search the premises.

I smiled—for *what* had I to fear? I bade the gentlemen welcome. The shriek, I said, was my own in a dream. The old man, I mentioned, was absent in the country. I took my visitors all over the house. I bade them search—search *well*. I led them, at length, to *his* chamber. I showed them his treasures, secure, undisturbed. In the enthusiasm of my confidence, I brought chairs into the room, and desired them *here* to rest from their fatigues, while I myself, in the wild audacity[5] of my perfect triumph, placed my own seat upon the very spot beneath which reposed the corpse of the victim.

The officers were satisfied. My *manner* had convinced them. I was singularly at ease. They sat, and while I answered cheerily, they chatted familiar things. But, ere long, I felt myself getting pale and wished them gone. My head ached, and I fancied a ringing in my ears: but still they sat and still chatted. The ringing became more distinct—it continued and became more distinct: I talked

---

5 audacity (ô das´ǝ tē): bold courage; daring.

more freely to get rid of the feeling: but it continued and gained definitiveness—until, at length, I found that the noise was *not* within my ears.

No doubt I now grew *very* pale—but I talked more fluently, and with a heightened voice. Yet the sound increased—and what could I do? It was *a low, dull, quick sound—much such a sound as a watch makes when enveloped in cotton.* I gasped for breath—and yet the officers heard it not. I talked more quickly—more vehemently; but the noise steadily increased. I arose and argued about trifles, in a high key and with violent gesticulations,[6] but the noise steadily increased. Why *would* they not be gone? I paced the floor to and fro with heavy strides, as if excited to fury by the observation of the men—but the noise steadily increased. Oh God! what *could* I do? I foamed—I raved—I swore! I swung the chair upon which I had been sitting, and grated it upon the boards, but the noise arose over all and continually increased. It grew louder—louder—*louder!* And still the men chatted pleasantly, and smiled. Was it possible they heard not? Almighty God!—no, no! They heard!—they suspected!—they *knew!*—they were making a mockery of my horror!—this I thought, and this I think. But anything was better than this agony! Anything was more tolerable than this derision![7] I could bear those hypocritical smiles no longer! I felt that I must scream or die!—and now—again!—hark! louder! louder! louder! *louder!*—

"Villains!" I shrieked, "dissemble[8] no more! I admit the deed!—tear up the planks!—here, here!—it is the beating of his hideous heart!"

---

6 gesticulations (jes tik´ yə lā´ shənz): gestures; movements of the hands and arms.

7 derision (di rizh´ən): mockery; ridicule.

8 dissemble (di sem´b´l): pretend.

THE
MONKEY'S
PAW

W. W. Jacobs

I

Without, the night was cold and wet, but in the small parlour of Laburnum Villa the blinds were drawn and the fire burned brightly. Father and son were at chess; the former, who possessed ideas about the game involving radical changes, putting his king into such sharp and unnecessary perils that it even provoked comment from the white-haired old lady knitting placidly by the fire.

"Hark at the wind," said Mr. White, who, having seen a fatal mistake after it was too late, was amiably desirous of preventing his son from seeing it.

"I'm listening," said the latter, grimly surveying the board as he stretched out his hand. "Check."

"I should hardly think that he'd come tonight," said his father, with his hand poised over the board.

"Mate," replied the son.

"That's the worst of living so far out," bawled Mr.

White, with sudden and unlooked-for violence; "of all the beastly, slushy, out-of-the-way places to live in, this is the worst. Path's a bog, and the road's a torrent. I don't know what people are thinking about. I suppose because only two houses in the road are let, they think it doesn't matter."

"Never mind, dear," said his wife soothingly; "perhaps you'll win the next one."

Mr. White looked up sharply, just in time to intercept a knowing glance between mother and son. The words died away on his lips, and he hid a guilty grin in his thin grey beard.

"There he is," said Herbert White, as the gate banged to loudly and heavy footsteps came toward the door.

The old man rose with hospitable haste, and opening the door, was heard condoling with the new arrival. The new arrival also condoled with himself, so that Mrs. White said, "Tut, tut!" and coughed gently as her husband entered the room, followed by a tall, burly man, beady of eye and rubicund of visage.

"Sergeant-Major Morris," he said, introducing him.

The sergeant-major shook hands, and taking the proffered seat by the fire, watched contentedly while his host got out whisky and tumblers and stood a small copper kettle on the fire.

At the third glass his eyes got brighter, and he began to talk, the little family circle regarding with eager interest this visitor from distant parts, as he squared his broad shoulders in the chair and spoke of wild scenes and doughty deeds; of wars and plagues and strange peoples.

"Twenty-one years of it," said Mr. White, nodding at his wife and son. "When he went away he was a slip of a youth in the warehouse. Now look at him."

"He don't look to have taken much harm," said Mrs. White politely.

"I'd like to go to India myself," said the old man, "just to look round a bit, you know."

"Better where you are," said the sergeant-major, shaking his head. He put down the empty glass, and sighing softly, shook it again.

"I should like to see those old temples and fakirs and jugglers," said the old man. "What was that you started telling me the other day about a monkey's paw or something, Morris?"

"Nothing," said the soldier hastily. "Leastways nothing worth hearing."

"Monkey's paw?" said Mrs. White curiously.

"Well, it's just a bit of what you might call magic, perhaps," said the sergeant-major offhandedly.

His three listeners leaned forward eagerly. The visitor absent-mindedly put his empty glass to his lips and then set it down again. His host filled it for him.

"To look at," said the sergeant-major, fumbling in his pocket, "it's just an ordinary little paw, dried to a mummy."

He took something out of his pocket and proffered it. Mrs. White drew back with a grimace, but her son, taking it, examined it curiously.

"And what is there special about it?" inquired Mr. White as he took it from his son, and having examined it, placed it upon the table.

"It had a spell put on it by an old fakir," said the sergeant-major, "a very holy man. He wanted to show that fate ruled people's lives, and that those who interfered with it did so to their sorrow. He put a spell on it so that three separate men could each have three wishes from it."

His manner was so impressive that his hearers were conscious that their light laughter jarred somewhat.

"Well, why don't you have three, sir?" said Herbert White cleverly.

The soldier regarded him in the way that middle age is wont to regard presumptuous youth. "I have," he said quietly, and his blotchy face whitened.

"And did you really have the three wishes granted?" asked Mrs. White.

"I did," said the sergeant-major, and his glass tapped against his strong teeth.

"And has anybody else wished?" persisted the old lady.

"The first man had his three wishes. Yes," was the reply; "I don't know what the first two were, but the third was for death. That's how I got the paw."

His tones were so grave that a hush fell upon the group.

"If you've had your three wishes, it's no good to you now, then, Morris," said the old man at last. "What do you keep it for?"

The soldier shook his head. "Fancy, I suppose," he said slowly. "I did have some idea of selling it, but I don't think I will. It has caused enough mischief already. Besides, people won't buy. They think it's a fairy tale, some of them; and those who do think anything of it want to try it first and pay me afterward."

"If you could have another three wishes," said the old man, eyeing him keenly, "would you have them?"

"I don't know," said the other. "I don't know."

He took the paw, and dangling it between his forefinger and thumb, suddenly threw it upon the fire. White, with a slight cry, stooped down and snatched it off.

"Better let it burn," said the soldier solemnly.

"If you don't want it, Morris," said the other, "give it to me."

"I won't," said his friend doggedly. "I threw it on the fire. If you keep it, don't blame me for what happens.

Pitch it on the fire again like a sensible man."

The other shook his head and examined his new possession closely. "How do you do it?" he inquired.

"Hold it up in your right hand and wish aloud," said the sergeant-major, "but I warn you of the consequences."

"Sounds like the *Arabian Nights*," said Mrs. White, as she rose and began to set the supper. "Don't you think you might wish for four pairs of hands for me?"

Her husband drew the talisman from his pocket, and then all three burst into laughter as the sergeant-major, with a look of alarm on his face, caught him by the arm.

"If you must wish," he said gruffly, "wish for something sensible."

Mr. White dropped it back in his pocket, and placing chairs, motioned his friend to the table. In the business of supper the talisman was partly forgotten, and afterward the three sat listening in an enthralled fashion to a second instalment of the soldier's adventures in India.

"If the tale about the monkey's paw is not more truthful than those he has been telling us," said Herbert, as the door closed behind their guest, just in time to catch the last train, "we shan't make much out of it."

"Did you give him anything for it, father?" inquired Mrs. White, regarding her husband closely.

"A trifle," said he, colouring slightly. "He didn't want it, but I made him take it. And he pressed me again to throw it away."

"Likely," said Herbert, with pretended horror. "Why we're going to be rich, and famous, and happy. Wish to be an emperor, father, to begin with; then you can't be henpecked."

He darted round the table, pursued by the maligned Mrs. White armed with an antimacassar.

Mr. White took the paw from his pocket and eyed it dubiously. "I don't know what to wish for, and that's a fact," he said slowly. "It seems to me I've got all I want."

"If you only cleared the house, you'd be quite happy, wouldn't you!" said Herbert, with his hand on his shoulder. "Well, wish for two hundred pounds, then; that'll just do it."

His father, smiling shamefacedly at his own credulity, held up the talisman, as his son, with a solemn face, somewhat marred by a wink at his mother, sat down at the piano and struck a few impressive chords.

"I wish for two hundred pounds," said the old man distinctly.

A fine crash from the piano greeted the words, interrupted by a shuddering cry from the old man. His wife and son ran toward him.

"It moved," he cried, with a glance of disgust at the object as it lay on the floor. "As I wished, it twisted in my hand like a snake."

"Well, I don't see the money," said his son, as he picked it up and placed it on the table, "and I bet I never shall."

"It must have been your fancy, father," said his wife, regarding him anxiously.

He shook his head. "Never mind, though; there's no harm done, but it gave me a shock all the same."

They sat down by the fire again while the two men finished their pipes. Outside, the wind was higher than ever, and the old man started nervously at the sound of a door banging upstairs. A silence unusual and depressing settled upon all three, which lasted until the old couple rose to retire for the night.

"I expect you'll find the cash tied up in a big bag in the middle of your bed," said Herbert, as he bade them good night, "and something horrible squatting up on top of the wardrobe watching you as you pocket your ill-gotten gains."

He sat alone in the darkness, gazing at the dying fire, and seeing faces in it. The last face was so horrible and so simian that he gazed at it in amazement. It got so vivid that, with a little uneasy laugh, he felt on the table for a glass containing a little water to throw over it. His hand grasped the monkey's paw, and with a little shiver he wiped his hand on his coat and went up to bed.

II

In the brightness of the wintry sun next morning as it streamed over the breakfast table he laughed at his fears. There was an air of prosaic wholesomeness about the room which it had lacked on the previous night, and the dirty, shrivelled little paw was pitched on the side-board with a carelessness which betokened no great belief in its virtues.

"I suppose all old soldiers are the same," said Mrs. White. "The idea of our listening to such nonsense! How could wishes be granted in these days? And if they could, how could two hundred pounds hurt you, father?"

"Might drop on his head from the sky," said the frivolous Herbert.

"Morris said the things happened so naturally," said his father, "that you might if you so wished attribute it to coincidence."

"Well, don't break into the money before I come back," said Herbert as he rose from the table. "I'm afraid it'll turn you into a mean, avaricious man, and we shall have to disown you."

His mother laughed, and following him to the door, watched him down the road; and returning to the breakfast table, was very happy at the expense of her husband's credulity. All of which did not prevent her from scurrying to the door at the postman's knock, nor prevent her from referring somewhat shortly to retired sergeant-majors of bibulous habits when she found that the post brought a tailor's bill.

"Herbert will have some more of his funny remarks, I expect, when he comes home," she said, as they sat at dinner.

"I dare say," said Mr. White, pouring himself out some beer; "but for all that, the thing moved in my hand; that I'll swear to."

"You thought it did," said the old lady, soothingly.

"I say it did," replied the other. "There was no thought about it; I had just—What's the matter?"

His wife made no reply. She was watching the mysterious movements of a man outside, who, peering in an undecided fashion at the house, appeared to be trying to make up his mind to enter. In mental connection with the two hundred pounds, she noticed that the stranger was well dressed, and wore a silk hat of glossy newness. Three times he paused at the gate, and then walked on again. The fourth time he stood with his hand upon it, and then with sudden resolution flung it open and walked up the path. Mrs. White at the same moment placed her hands behind her, and hurriedly unfastening the strings of her apron, put that useful article of apparel beneath the cushion of her chair.

She brought the stranger, who seemed ill at ease, into the room. He gazed at her furtively, and listened in a preoccupied fashion as the old lady apologized for the appearance of the room, and her husband's coat, a garment which he usually reserved for the garden. She then waited as patiently as she could for him to broach his business, but he was at first strangely silent.

"I—was asked to call," he said at last, and stooped and picked a piece of cotton from his trousers. "I come from 'Maw and Meggins'."

The old lady started. "Is anything the matter?" she asked breathlessly. "Has anything happened to Herbert? What is it? What is it?"

Her husband interposed. "There, there, mother," he said hastily. "Sit down, and don't jump to conclusions. You've not brought bad news, I'm sure, sir," and he eyed the other wistfully.

"I'm sorry—" began the visitor.

"Is he hurt?" demanded the mother wildly.

The visitor bowed in assent. "Badly hurt," he said quietly, "but he is not in any pain."

"Oh, thank God!" said the old woman, clasping her hands. "Thank God for that! Thank—"

She broke off suddenly as the sinister meaning of the assurance dawned upon her and she saw the awful confirmation of her fears in the other's averted face. She caught her breath, and turning to her slower-witted husband, laid her trembling old hand upon his. There was a long silence.

"He was caught in the machinery," said the visitor at length in a low voice.

"Caught in the machinery," repeated Mr. White, in a dazed fashion, "yes."

He sat staring blankly out at the window, and taking his wife's hand between his own, pressed it as he had been wont to do in their old courting days nearly forty years before.

"He was the only one left to us," he said, turning gently to the visitor. "It is hard."

The other coughed, and rising, walked slowly to the window. "The firm wished me to convey their sincere sympathy with you in your great loss," he said, without looking round. "I beg that you will understand I am only their servant and merely obeying orders."

There was no reply; the old woman's face was white, her eyes staring, and her breath inaudible; on the husband's face was a look such as his friend the sergeant might have carried into his first action.

"I was to say that Maw and Meggins disclaim all responsibility," continued the other. "They admit no liability at all, but in consideration of your son's services, they wish to present you with a certain sum as compensation."

Mr. White dropped his wife's hand, and rising to his feet, gazed with a look of horror at his visitor. His dry lips shaped the words, "How much?"

"Two hundred pounds," was the answer.

Unconscious of his wife's shriek, the old man smiled faintly, put out his hands like a sightless man, and dropped, a senseless heap, to the floor.

III

In the huge new cemetery, some two miles distant, the old people buried their dead, and came back to the house steeped in shadow and silence. It was all over so quickly that at first they could hardly realize it, and remained in a state of expectation as though of something else to happen—something else which was to lighten this load, too heavy for old hearts to bear.

But the days passed, and expectation gave place to resignation—the hopeless resignation of the old, sometimes miscalled apathy. Sometimes they hardly exchanged a word, for now they had nothing to talk about, and their days were long to weariness.

It was about a week after that the old man, waking suddenly in the night, stretched out his hand and found himself alone. The room was in darkness, and the sound of subdued weeping came from the window. He raised himself in bed and listened.

"Come back," he said tenderly. "You will be cold."

"It is colder for my son," said the old woman, and wept afresh.

The sound of her sobs died away on his ears. The bed was warm, and his eyes heavy with sleep. He dozed fitfully, and then slept until a sudden wild cry from his wife awoke him with a start.

"*The paw!*" she cried wildly. "The monkey's paw!"

He started up in alarm. "Where? Where is it? What's the matter?"

She came stumbling across the room toward him. "I want it," she said quietly. "You've not destroyed it?"

"It's in the parlour, on the bracket," he replied, marvelling. "Why?"

She cried and laughed together, and bending over, kissed his cheek.

"I only just thought of it," she said hysterically. "Why didn't I think of it before? Why didn't *you* think of it?"

"Think of what?" he questioned.

"The other two wishes," she replied rapidly. "We've only had one."

"Was not that enough?" he demanded fiercely.

"No," she cried triumphantly; "we'll have one more. Go down and get it quickly, and wish our boy alive again."

The man sat up in bed and flung the bedclothes from his quaking limbs. "Good God, you are mad!" he cried, aghast.

"Get it," she panted; "get it quickly, and wish—Oh, my boy, my boy!"

Her husband struck a match and lit the candle. "Get back to bed," he said unsteadily. "You don't know what you are saying."

"We had the first wish granted," said the old woman feverishly, "why not the second?"

"A coincidence," stammered the old man.

"Go and get it and wish," cried his wife, quivering with excitement.

The old man turned and regarded her, and his voice shook. "He has been dead ten days, and besides he— I would not tell you else, but—I could only recognize him by his clothing. If he was too terrible for you to see then, how now?"

"Bring him back," cried the old woman, and dragged him toward the door. "Do you think I fear the child I have nursed?"

He went down in the darkness, and felt his way to the parlour, and then to the mantelpiece. The talisman was in its place, and a horrible fear that the unspoken wish might bring his mutilated son before him ere he could escape from the room seized upon him, and he caught his breath as he found that he had lost the direction of the door. His brow cold with sweat, he felt his way round the table, and groped along the wall until he found himself in the small passage with the unwholesome thing in his hand.

Even his wife's face seemed changed as he entered the room. It was white and expectant, and to his fears seemed to have an unnatural look upon it. He was afraid of her.

"*Wish!*" she cried, in a strong voice.

"It is foolish and wicked," he faltered.

"*Wish!*" repeated his wife.

He raised his hand. "I wish my son alive again."

The talisman fell to the floor, and he regarded it fearfully. Then he sank trembling into a chair as the old woman, with burning eyes, walked to the window and raised the blind.

He sat until he was chilled with the cold, glancing occasionally at the figure of the old woman peering through the window. The candle-end, which had burned below the rim of the china candlestick, was throwing pulsating shadows on the ceiling and walls, until, with a flicker larger than the rest, it expired. The old man, with an unspeakable sense of relief at the failure of the talisman, crept back to his bed, and a minute or two afterward the old woman came silently and apathetically beside him.

Neither spoke, but lay silently listening to the ticking of the clock. A stair creaked, and a squeaky mouse scurried noisily through the wall. The darkness was oppressive, and after lying for some time screwing up his courage, he took the box of matches, and striking one, went downstairs for a candle.

At the foot of the stairs the match went out, and he paused to strike another; and at the same moment a knock, so quiet and stealthy as to be scarcely audible, sounded on the front door.

The matches fell from his hand and spilled in the passage. He stood motionless, his breath suspended until the knock was repeated. Then he turned and fled swiftly back to his room, and closed the door behind him. A third knock sounded through the house.

"*What's that?*" cried the old woman, starting up.

"A rat," said the old man in shaking tones—"a rat. It passed me on the stairs."

His wife sat up in bed listening. A loud knock resounded through the house.

"It's Herbert!" she screamed. "It's Herbert!"

She ran to the door, but her husband was before her, and catching her by the arm, held her tightly.

"What are you going to do?" he whispered hoarsely.

"It's my boy; it's Herbert!" she cried, struggling mechanically. "I forgot it was two miles away. What are you holding me for? Let go. I must open the door."

"For God's sake don't let it in," cried the old man, trembling.

"You're afraid of your own son," she cried, struggling. "Let me go. I'm coming Herbert; I'm coming."

There was another knock, and another. The old woman with a sudden wrench broke free and ran from the room. Her husband followed to the landing, and called after her appealingly as she hurried downstairs. He heard the chain rattle back and the bottom bolt drawn slowly and stiffly from the socket. Then the old woman's voice, strained and panting.

"The bolt," she cried loudly. "Come down, I can't reach it."

But her husband was on his hands and knees groping wildly on the floor in search of the paw. If he could only find it before the thing outside got in. A perfect fusillade of knocks reverberated through the house, and he heard the scraping of a chair as his wife put it down in the passage against the door. He heard the creaking of the bolt as it came slowly back, and at the same moment he found the monkey's paw, and frantically breathed his third and last wish.

The knocking ceased suddenly, although the echoes of it were still in the house. He heard the chair drawn back, and the door opened. A cold wind rushed up the staircase, and a long loud wail of disappointment and misery from his wife gave him courage to run down to her side, and then to the gate beyond. The street lamp flickering opposite shone on a quiet and deserted road.

Manerathiak's Song

Kamaoktunga . . . I am afraid and I tremble
When I remember my father and mother
Seeking the wandering game,
Struggling on the empty land
Weakened by hunger. *Eya-ya-ya* . . .

Kamaoktunga . . . I am afraid and I tremble
When I recall their bones
Scattered on the low land,
Broken by prowling beasts,
Swept away by winds. *Eya-ya-ya* . . .

The Wind Has Wings

Nunaptigne . . . In our land—*ahe, ahe, ee, ee, iee*—
The wind has wings, winter and summer.
It comes by night and it comes by day,
And children must fear it—*ahe, ahe, ee, ee, iee.*
In our land the nights are long,
And the spirits like to roam in the dark.
I've seen their faces, I've seen their eyes.
They are like ravens, hovering over the dead,
Their dark wings forming long shadows,
And children must fear them—*ahe, ahe, ee, ee, iee.*

INUIT CHANTS
TRANSLATED BY RAYMOND DE COCCOLA
AND PAUL KING

Witchcraft was hung, in History

Witchcraft was hung, in History,
But History and I
Find all the Witchcraft that we need
Around us, every Day—

EMILY DICKINSON

Something Is There

Something is there
   there on the stair
      coming down
         coming down
            stepping with care.
          Coming down
           coming down
              slinkety-sly.

Something is coming and wants to get by.

LILIAN MOORE

Thirty Below

The prairie wind sounds colder
than any wind I have ever heard.
Looking through frosted windows
I see snow whirl in the street
and think how deep
all over the country now
snow drifts
and cars are stuck
on icy roads.
A solitary man walking
wraps his face in a woollen mask,
turns his back sometimes
so as not to front
this biting, eye-smarting wind.
Suddenly I see my dead father
in an old coat too thin for him,
the tabs of his cap pulled over his ears,
on a drifted road in New Brunswick
walking with bowed head
towards home.

ELIZABETH BREWSTER

VISIT TO THE
"TWILIGHT ZONE"
TRUCK STOP

by Phyllis Griffiths
introduction by John R. Columbo

"*Visit to the 'Twilight Zone' Truck Stop" is my title
for this account of an eerie experience. The experience
itself recalls the decade of the Sixties in such detail that
the experience might well have been an episode on Rod
Serling's long-running "Twilight Zone" television series.*

*Yet the event that sparked the shared experience
occurred not in the 1960s but in the year 1978. It happened to Phyllis and Don Griffiths. Mrs. Griffiths sent
me this account after she heard me talk about "extraordi-
nary experiences" on CFAX Radio in Victoria, B.C.*

*"I have a story that you may wish to add to your files
of strange experiences," she explained in her letter of 27
March 1989. "My husband and I refer to this as our
'twilight zone' visit. If it was a hallucination, then it is
one that we both shared. The story is enclosed with this
letter."*

Here it is. Sky Chief indeed!

In March of 1978, we were returning to our home in Lethbridge, Alberta, after spending Easter Week visiting relatives on Vancouver Island. This was a trip that the family had taken many times before, and the route we usually followed was first along Highway 1, the northern route, and then south from Calgary. This time, we decided, just for a change of pace, that we would take Highway 3. We had not taken this southern highway before when returning from Vancouver Island.

As usual with return trips, this one was to be driven straight through. But the route was unfamiliar to us, and the southern route was taking much longer than the familiar northern route. Our two young sons slept cuddled up to their dog in the back seat of the family station wagon. My husband and I drove through the night and into the early hours of the next day without a rest.

At two-thirty in the morning we drove into the town of Creston, B.C. The only place open at that early hour was a tiny service station, where we stopped to refuel the car. Tired as we were, we had no choice but to drive on. There was no money for a motel room, nor were there camp-grounds in the area.

Relief was found about half way between Creston and Cranbrook. It took the form of an old Texaco Truck Stop which we were approaching. It was on the north side of the highway, Highway 3, but it was located in the middle of nowhere. It was a totally unexpected sight, but a very welcome one.

The Texaco Truck Stop had an unusual location, but it also had an unusual appearance. The large old Texaco sign was a solid sign lit by spotlights mounted on top and focused on the painted surface. The gas pumps were also old-fashioned looking, and they dispensed good old Fire Chief and Sky Chief gasoline. There was a diesel pump at the side, but no pumps for unleaded gas were in sight.

The station itself looked as if it had not changed one bit since the year 1960. Even the semi-trailer unit, idling in the truck lot to one side, was of an early Sixties vintage. Everything looked strange indeed. Was this a scene from Rod Serling's "Twilight Zone"?

Nevertheless, my husband and I, tired and thirsty as we were, drove in, pulled up under the pump lights, got out of the car, and locked it. We left our two children asleep in the back seat of the car.

The inside of the restaurant matched the outside to such a degree that everything felt spooky. The interior was frozen in time in the year 1960, yet the decor showed none of the wear and tear that would be found after nearly twenty years of use. We could see nothing that was out of place. There was nothing new or modern about the appointments or the personnel. The waitress was dressed in period clothes, as was the driver of the semi parked in the yard.

The price of the coffee was all of a dime a cup, and a placard advertised the price of a piece of pie as a quarter. The music blaring from the radio dated from the late Fifties, and the d.j. introduced the songs without once referring to the period or to any item of news. No calendar was in sight. But the coffee was good and was appreciated. We felt uneasy in the place, so we were not unhappy to be out and on the road for home once more.

We had driven this stretch of Highway 3 on previous occasions, but it had always been in daylight and heading in the other direction. We had never taken it at night or while returning from Vancouver Island. We had memorized the location of every truck stop on Highway 3, and we thought we knew the location of all the truck stops that were open twenty-four hours a day on this highway as well. But never before had we seen this one. Nor did we ever see it again.

The visit left us with an eerie feeling. Try as we might, we could not shake it off. We asked those of our friends and relatives who occasionally travelled that stretch of Highway 3 if they were familiar with the old Texaco Truck Stop. No one knew anything about it. Everyone was of the opinion that there was no such establishment between Lethbridge, Alta., and Hope, B.C.

The only thing that we could do was re-drive that stretch of highway in broad daylight and watch out for it to see for ourselves whether or not the place really existed. Some months later we did just that. We retravelled Highway 3. Mid-way between Cranbrook and Creston, on the north side of the road, we found the place where we had stopped that eerie night.

The building had long been boarded over. The presence of the pumps was marked only by their cement bases. The same was true of the Texaco signpost. The yard where the semi had sat was overgrown with bush and with aspen poplars which were twenty or more feet in height. It had been many years since that particular service station had pumped gas or served coffee at a dime a cup. But my husband and I know that the old Truck Stop had been open for business that lonely March night in 1978, when a weary family had stopped—in need of a cup of coffee and a bit of rest.

About the Authors

T. Ernesto Bethancourt (1932–) did not start writing books for young people until he was forty-one. His first children's book is an autobiography written for his daughter.

William Blake (1757–1827), an Englishman, was not only a poet but also an engraver, a painter, and a mystic. He used his own engravings and watercolours to illustrate his work.

Arna Bontemps (1902–1974) pursued writing against the wishes of his father. In addition to poetry and novels, Bontemps wrote many books for children; he felt children were more sensitive to injustice than adults.

Ray Bradbury (1920–) first published his fantasy and science fiction stories in pulp magazines and only later became known as a serious writer. His stories range in mood from macabre to humorous.

Elizabeth Brewster (1922–) began writing poetry as a way of working through her problems. Today, forty years later, this Canadian author continues to write poetry as well as novels and short stories.

Wayson Choy grew up in Vancouver, and he has drawn upon the traits of some of the people in his childhood to create the imaginary characters in "Jade Peony." In his writing Choy enjoys creating wonder not found in the logical world.

Charles de Lint was born in 1951 and became a Canadian citizen in 1961. He is best known for his contemporary fantasy stories, but he also writes critically acclaimed novels that blend fantasy, horror, and suspense.

Emily Dickinson (1830–1886) lived a quiet, reclusive life in Amherst, Massachusetts. Although only seven of her 1775 poems were published in her lifetime, today she is recognized as a major American poet.

T. S. Eliot (1888–1965) ranks as one of the most important poets of the twentieth century. Eliot is known for his bizarre imagery and ability to express the fearful aspects of mundane experiences.

Susan Glaspell (1876–1948) began her career by writing romances with "happily ever after" endings. Later, she turned to writing plays, novels, and stories that explore people's awareness of the flaws in contemporary society.

Phyllis Griffiths didn't set out to write about the unexplained. "Visit to the 'Twilight Zone' Truck Stop" originated as a letter in response to a Victoria, B.C., radio talk show about odd occurrences. Griffiths simply wanted to share her experience.

Langston Hughes (1902–1967) expresses in his poetry the despair of urban American blacks. His poetry is not bleak, however, but is instead tempered by Hughes's wonderful sense of humor.

W. W. Jacobs (1863–1943) wrote nineteen volumes of short stories, most of which are about sailors' adventures. Ironically, his most famous work, "The Monkey's Paw," doesn't feature sailors or the sea.

Ronald Keon is a contemporary Canadian poet of Algonquin, Iroquois, and Irish heritage.

Cheryl MacDonald (1952–) is a historical writer who has recently finished a manuscript for a book on the Olive Sternaman case. MacDonald lives in the very same county in Canada where the case took place.

Eve Merriam (1916–1992) worked as a poet, biographer, radio writer, fashion-magazine editor, and teacher. Her poetry has won many honors and awards.

Lilian Moore began her career as a teacher. Frustrated by the lack of good children's books for her students, she began to write her own. Moore now has over forty books to her credit, some of which have been adapted for film.

Phillipa Pearce (1920–) is best known for her story *Tom's Midnight Garden*, a fantasy about what happens when a boy discovers a mysterious garden after he hears a clock strike thirteen.

Edgar Allan Poe (1809–1849), orphaned at the age of two, was taken into the home of a Richmond merchant, John Allan. Although Poe wrote poetry, he is best known for his terrifying and suspenseful short stories.

Theodore Roethke (1908–1963) described his adolescence as a time of insecurity and loneliness. In the course of his self-discovery, Roethke became an outstanding poet and won many awards and honors, including the Pulitzer Prize for poetry in 1954.

Leslie Marmon Silko, born in 1948 in Albuquerque, New Mexico, explores her Native American heritage in her stories and poems. She says that her ethnic background frames her identity as a writer.

Edwin Varney is a contemporary Canadian poet whose work has appeared in *New West Coast*, an anthology of western Canadian poetry.

Credits

1 "The Jade Peony" was first published in the UBC Alumni Chronicle. Copyright © 1979 by Wayson Choy. Used by permission of the author.

12 Reprinted by permission of Harold Ober Associates Incorporated. Copyright © 1963 by Arna Bontemps.

13 From "Was It Murder?" by Cheryl MacDonald from *The Beaver Magazine*, October/November 1991. Reprinted by permission of the author.

26 From *Plays* by Susan Glaspell. Copyright © 1920 by Dodd, Mead & Company. Published by Dodd, Mead & Company.

46 Reprinted by permission of Richard Curtis Associates, Inc.

55 From *Who's Afraid and Other Strange Stories* by Philippa Pearce. Copyright © 1988 by Philippa Pearce, Puffin Books. Reprinted by permission of the author and Laura Cecil Literary Agency.

69 Appeared in *Aladdin and Other Tales from The Arabian Nights* retold by N.J. Dawood. Copyright © 1973 by N.J. Dawood. Published by the Penguin Group. Reprinted by permission of N.J. Dawood.

71 From *The Storyteller* by Leslie Marmon Silko. Copyright © 1981 by Leslie Marmon Silko. Reprinted by permission of Wylie, Aitken & Stone.

74 "Reach out..." reprinted by permission of the author.

74 "Landscape" from A SKY FULL OF POEMS by Eve Merriam. Copyright © 1964, 1970, 1973 by Eve Merriam. Reprinted by permission of Marian Reiner, Permissions Consultant.

75 From *Old Possum's Book of Practical Cats* by T.S. Eliot. Copyright © 1939 by T.S. Eliot. Published by Faber & Faber Limited.

77 Copyright © 1938 by Theodore Roethke. From *The Collected Poems of Theodore Roethke* by Theodore Roethke. Used by permission of Doubleday, a division of Bantam Doubleday Dell Publishing Group, Inc.

77 Poem by Southwest Tribes appeared in *Experiencing Poetry* edited by Eileen Thompson. Copyright © 1987 by Eileen Thompson. Published by Globe Book Company, Inc.

79 Both poems from *Selected Poems of Langston Hughes* by Langston Hughes. Copyright 1947 by Langston Hughes. Reprinted by permission of Alfred A. Knopf, Inc.

80 "User Friendly" by T. Ernesto Bethancourt, copyright © 1989 by T. Ernesto Bethancourt, from *Connections: Short Stories by Outstanding Writers for Young Adults* by Donald R. Gallo, Editor. Used by permission of Delacorte Press, a division of Bantam Doubleday Dell Publishing Group, Inc.

94 Reprinted by permission of Don Congdon Associates, Inc. Copyright © 1951, renewed 1979 by Ray Bradbury.